M000314823

"One might expect a b[...] cancer, and the hand of God to be comprised of the sappy platitudes and euphemisms that fill the pages of the kind of 'inspiration porn' that litters the shelves of the parenting section of your local bookseller. This book is decidedly NOT that.

This is the story of a scrappy, devoted, and self-deprecating couple who refused to pretend everything was 'just fine' at the same time they refused to give up on joy, love, and humor in the face of chronic challenges. Clay's narration demonstrates that joy, gratitude, anger, grief, celebration—even double entendres—and Christianity are not mutually exclusive. More than that, it lays bare one man's unshakeable devotion to and gratitude for the four women who powerfully shaped his life— Carole, Blaire, Paige, and Mia."

—**Sara Gelser Blouin**, Oregon State Senator
Former Member, National Council on Disability

"Cancer, disabilities, death . . . followed by months of isolated quarantine and lost in the depths of deep grief. Where do you find hope when unrelenting hardships have invaded, and you're stumbling through the splintered remains of shattered dreams?

You saturate your soul in the words of this book, *God's Plan, Our Circus*. Clay is unapologetically honest, unquestionably reassuring as he weaves humor and humility throughout the pages. I pray his words provide hope as you rebuild your life, renew your trust in God. As Clay will tell you, God will redeem your pain; watch His good plan unfold!"

—**Colleen Swindoll-Thompson**,
Vice President, Insight for Living
Founder, Reframing Ministries

"Saturated with wisdom and humor, *God's Plan, Our Circus* is a well-written adventure taking us through the tangible trials of life. Clay Boatright clinched the undeniable emotions for a passionate and driven follower of Christ walking through tragedy and unexpected heartbreak. Clay conveys his wealth of wisdom and credibility as an advocate in his role as a husband, father, and servant leader. This book is profound and exudes courage and hope in the midst of doubt."

—Ronald Brown, Executive Pastor, Shoreline City Church
Past President, The Arc of the United States

"Early in Clay Boatright's credo, he describes an *ah-hah!* moment where he accepts that his sole purpose is to care for family. He didn't realize his steps would go far beyond his cherished wife and daughters.

As a disability advocate, I always wanted his strong voice in our mission. Clay didn't take no for an answer, and his passionate and committed leadership continues to benefit many thousands of people with disabilities. Readers need not be spiritual or have experience with disability to find the moral compass in Clay's journey."

—Dennis Borel, Executive Director,
Coalition of Texans with Disabilities

"It was a pleasure reading this book. I love the humor and the faith-based perspective that permeated every story. Being a parent of an adult son with autism, I can appreciate how much faith and humor are needed, otherwise it can be very overwhelming. The book is well written, easy to read, and interesting. One of my favorite things about the book is the highlighted lessons learned. They are wonderful insights to live by."

—Nagla N. Moussa, Founder,
National Autism Association of North Texas

"If the title doesn't grab you, the life in these pages will. *God's Plan, Our Circus* is a lasting memoir of a man who found ways to understand, remain relevant, and stay true to a God calling that most would swear they would never do—and most will never face. If you believe and think you're mentally incapable, unable to endure, and won't be able to handle something in life, most likely you won't. Clay's words treat us to facing what 'never, always, and most likely' may be for real, but he devotes huge sections of writing to the core needs within any man or woman who wants to deepen ideas of faith, mental health, and advocacy in their life.

What was profoundly the most helpful and meaningful to me as Licensed Professional Counselor, were the unspoken ways Clay indirectly and succinctly grasped how wide, deep, and far the love of Christ (Ephesians 3:18) may be for him or any human in any manner of pain or circumstances. I highly recommend reading in full the entirety of this book, no matter what your own reference point for pain may be. You may either find a friend in its pages or a new lease on life from one who is still pursuing life fully.

—Andrew Siefers, MA,
Licensed Professional Counselor Supervisor

GOD'S PLAN, OUR CIRCUS

GOD'S PLAN, OUR CIRCUS

A FAMILY ODYSSEY THROUGH AUTISM, DEATH, AND REINVENTION

CLAY BOATRIGHT

Stonebrook Publishing
Saint Louis, Missouri

A STONEBROOK PUBLISHING BOOK
©2023 Clay Boatright

This book was guided in development and
edited by Nancy L. Erickson, The Book Professor®
TheBookProfessor.com

All Scripture quotations, unless otherwise indicated, are taken from
the Holy Bible, New International Version®, NIV®. Copyright ©1973,
1978, 1984, 2011 by Biblica, Inc.™ Used by permission of Zondervan.
All rights reserved worldwide. www.zondervan.com The "NIV" and
"New International Version" are trademarks registered in the United
States Patent and Trademark Office by Biblica, Inc.™

Library of Congress Control Number: 2022919505

ISBN: 978-1-955711-22-7
eBook ISBN: 978-1-955711-23-4

www.stonebrookpublishing.net

PRINTED IN THE UNITED STATES OF AMERICA

For a powerhouse girl from Memphis,
Carole Beall Boatright, and our three daughters,
whom she loved more than life itself—
Blaire, Paige, and Mia.

CONTENTS

PROLOGUE

"PLEASE FILL OUT THESE FORMS, and the doctor will be in soon," our pediatrician's nurse told us at the twenty-four-month well-baby visit.

"Can walk downstairs while holding hands" and "Uses words like me, I, or you" were two of the twenty-five statements on each form. Carole held Paige and filled it out while I did the same for Mia. We completed the forms, looked at each other, and our stomachs churned. Neither one of us had checked off anything.

"There seems to be something going on here," our doctor told us. "I think you should go to Easter Seals for an evaluation."

Easter Seals? I thought that was for children in wheelchairs.

"They are clearly behind their two-year-old peers," the Easter Seals' director said. "I think that developmental gap is going to increase."

"What do they have?" Carole asked as tears formed in her eyes.

"I hate to diagnose at this early age," the doctor replied. "Labels can be detrimental to children as they grow, and it really won't affect your course of action."

"That's bull!" I shouted. "You said our children will not develop normally. What do you think is wrong?"

She saw the anger in my eyes and knew she had to shoot straight.

"If I had to make a diagnosis today," she said as the tension in the room mounted, "I would say they have intellectual disabilities and probably autism as well."

1

YOUNG AND STUPID

"**U**MM, THAT'S MY BUTT!" laughed the cute twenty-year-old blonde with big eighties hair. Carole sat on her girlfriend's lap in the passenger seat of my 1979 Mazda RX-7, a car barely big enough for one person, much less three.

"Sorry, I was reaching for my stick," I smiled, curious if an innuendo about manual transmission would get a response.

In August 1986, I was twenty-one, fresh out of grad school, and still living in my hometown of Memphis, Tennessee. Teri, our mutual friend, had invited me to dinner at Pizza Hut so I could meet Carole. I sat with my back to the wall when she walked in. *Oh my!* I thought. *She really is pretty!*

I dropped Carole at home and planned a date with her for that weekend. Full of excitement on Friday night, I called before walking out the door.

"Ya know; I just got home from work, and I'm exhausted," she said. "Can we go out some other time?"

"Sure, I understand," I replied. "I hope you feel better."

Back in a T-shirt to watch *Family Ties*, I felt crushed and alone. Nobody ever stood up Michael J. Fox on a first date. One thing was for sure: that girl would not get asked out again.

A few days later, Teri said that Carole felt bad for canceling our evening. My firm decision to never ask her out again was quickly thrown out the window, and I called her that night.

"Would you like to go to the fair?" she asked.

"The Mid-South Fair?" I replied with surprise. "I haven't been to the fair in years. If that's where you want to go, let's do it!"

We walked hand in hand through the fairgrounds, rode the Zippin' Pippin roller coaster, and dined on Pronto Pup corn dogs. A few hours into the night, we spotted a photo booth and popped in for a picture button. We looked like two babies who'd escaped from their cribs. Picture buttons taken at local fairs and festivals every autumn would chronicle our lives for the next twenty years.

"MOST OF MY CLASSES ARE IN THE MORNING," Carole, now my steady girlfriend for about a year, said on the phone one afternoon. She was starting her senior year at Memphis State and received her class schedule. "I have one class that meets on Tuesday nights."

Ever since grad school, I taught an undergrad marketing class each semester. As coincidence would have it, my class met on Tuesday evenings as well.

"That's convenient," I replied. "What class is it?"

"Trade Promotion 2104," she answered.

The long pause caught her attention.

"You're not going to believe this," I replied, "but I'm teaching that class!" We both laughed, knowing this could get weird.

For four months, only one mutual friend, who was another student in the class, knew that the teacher was Carole's boyfriend. While her classwork may not have been stellar, Carole earned her A.

After graduation, Carole got a sales job with AT&T that required her to go to training in Cincinnati for three weeks. We talked every night, which made the time go by fast. When she came home, I was ready to take our relationship to a new level.

"I'll be right back," I told Carole as we finished dinner at Bennigan's one night. "I need to run to the restroom."

This is it, thought the guy in the bathroom mirror. *Everything is about to change. You don't need to do it. You can take the ring back where you bought it, and she'll never know.*

"Oh my God, YES!" Carole exclaimed when I opened the ring box. Her excitement caught the attention of our server.

"Congratulations! We'll give you a free dessert to celebrate!" he said. "Are you two the same religion?"

We nodded yes, but it wasn't true. I was a BINO (Baptist in Name Only) and would walk into a church maybe once every couple of years. Carole and her Methodist parents, on the other hand, sat on the third pew every Sunday, a practice she and I adopted when we married.

Almost twenty years later, I was alone in a hospital room with Richard, Carole's father. There was something I needed to tell him.

"Thank you for raising your daughter in the church," I said. "I followed your example, and it brought me closer to Christ. I'm not sure that would have happened had I not married Carole."

"I appreciate that," Richard replied. He passed away four days later. I may not have been the world's best son-in-law, but I wanted him to know his life-changing impact on me.

CAROLE AND I HAD BEEN MARRIED FOR A YEAR when we drove to her parents' house for a conversation we dreaded.

"We have some news," I said as we sat in their living room. "I've been offered a job in Saint Louis, and we're going to move in a few weeks."

You could have heard a pin drop as they looked at us in complete silence. They'd lived in Memphis most of their lives, and I was about to take their only child away from them.

"There are jobs in Memphis," Richard said. "Why don't you get one here?"

"In my line of work," I explained, "getting ahead often means having to move."

His follow-up question caught us off guard. "Who's going to take care of us if we get sick?" he asked.

Carole and I sat stunned

"We'll always make sure you're okay," Carole said. "We're just moving a few hours up the road. We'll still see each other all the time."

She and I promised each other that night that we'd never make our children feel guilty. We also agreed our happiness would never be based on the decisions of others.

WE ALSO AGREED OUR HAPPINESS
WOULD NEVER BE BASED ON THE
DECISIONS OF OTHERS.

"This job isn't what I thought it would be," I told my father six months later. "Do you think we made the right decision to move?"

My dad was a quiet man who believed people should listen more often than speak. At that moment, he looked at me as though I had lost my mind.

"Of course, you made the right decision," he replied. "It's the right decision because it was the decision you made. You weighed the options and did what you felt was right for your family. If things change down the road, then you can make a new decision, but never second-guess yourself."

Dad's affirmation made a deep impact. From that day on, I never second-guessed myself or thought about what-ifs after the fact. Second-guessing is a worthless mental game that makes us miserable as we envision a happier life out of our reach. We forget bad things could happen on the other path as well. There's a psychological term for that pain-free, what-if life we envision. It's called a fantasy.

SECOND-GUESSING IS A WORTHLESS
MENTAL GAME THAT MAKES US MISERABLE
AS WE ENVISION A HAPPIER LIFE
OUT OF OUR REACH.

"IS THERE ANYTHING IN PARTICULAR I SHOULD KNOW ABOUT?" the doctor asked Carole at the end of her first appointment after we'd moved to Saint Louis.

"Well, this strange bump showed up on my collarbone," she answered, as she pointed to a spot on her neck.

"It's probably nothing, but you don't need a bump on your collarbone. Let's make an appointment to remove it, and we'll run a biopsy to make sure it's okay," he recommended.

Our first "adulting moment" happened two weeks later when I answered the phone in my work cube.

"You need to come home now," Carole said with panic in her voice. "I have cancer."

That bump turned out to be Stage II-B Hodgkin's Lymphoma, a cancer of the lymph nodes.

"We can do radiation or chemotherapy," the oncologist explained on our first visit. "Radiation may not get all of it, so then we'd have to do chemo too. Meanwhile, we know the chemo will knock it out."

"That's easy," Carole told him without hesitation. "Let's do chemo and be done with it."

"I agree," the doctor replied. "We need a bone marrow biopsy to make sure it hasn't gone there. We can do it right now if you have time."

The doctor led us down the hall of the HMO office building to a room that had only a table. Carole changed into a hospital gown and climbed up as a flow of people entered the room.

"Are all these people necessary for this?" I asked a middle-aged man in a white doctor's coat. By now, at least a dozen folks crowded around Carole on the table.

"No, but we've never seen this done in an office before," he replied. I didn't tell Carole that she was that day's office guinea pig.

The oncologist came back with two syringes, a small one for local anesthetic and a gigantic one for the elephant that must have been in the parking lot. He gave Carole the small shot in her hip, then stuck the sword of the other into the same spot. It hit the bone, and the doctor cranked it like uncorking a bottle of wine. He twisted, twisted, and twisted again. As Carole screamed into a towel, liquid filled the tube, followed by bone marrow that floated in the juice like a worm in a tequila bottle.

"How are you feeling?" I asked Carole two weeks later as she lay on a hospital bed at the HMO. Chemicals flowed into the Groshong catheter that stuck three inches out of her chest.

"It's been a couple of hours, and it's not too bad," she replied.

"That's good. Scoot over. I'm climbing in," I said as she moved over to the edge of the bed. Like a good husband, I gave her a kiss to make her feel better.

"What did you eat for lunch?" Carole asked with an unpleasant look on her face.

"A tuna sandwich at the café downstairs," I replied.

She rolled to the other side of the bed and vomited on the floor. My work here was done.

"I don't want to lose my hair," Carole said on the way home. The doctor predicted it would fall out on day twenty, and the clock started that first day of chemo.

"Bald is beautiful!" I responded. "Look at Grace Jones or that bald alien chick in the *Star Trek* movie. You women obsess about your hair, but hot is hot, bald or not!"

Nineteen days later, my work phone rang again.

"Sure as shit, it's day twenty," Carole laughed. "I brushed my hair when I got out of the shower, and it's coming out in gobs!"

When I got home that night, she handed me the scissors and said, "Finish the job!" A final once-over with an electric shaver and her head was as smooth as a baby's butt.

It was important for Carole's white blood counts to remain strong, and if they dropped into the danger zone, we packed a bag for the hospital. One morning we were in her hospital room when a doctor walked in with an entourage of junior white coats. He made technical observations, using scary words we didn't understand, then asked Carole if she had any questions.

"I'm not going to die, am I?" she asked as her voice quivered.

"Well, I don't think so, but we never know for sure," he replied in a cold, monotone voice. I was shocked beyond belief.

When the crowd left Carole's room, I followed Dr. Board Certified to the nurses' station. This brash twenty-six-year-old husband looked him dead in the eye and unleashed a volcanic fury.

"What the hell is wrong with you?" I shouted for the whole floor to hear. "I don't care how smart you are; your bedside manner sucks. You don't tell someone being treated for one of the most curable cancers that you don't know if she's going to die or not!"

"I didn't want to lie to her," he replied, annoyed by this commoner.

"Horse shit! You could have said, 'Anything can happen, but you'll be fine. You're in great hands.' That would have been honest and not dashed her hope."

The nurses behind the desk smiled. It must have made an impact because when Doc dropped by the next day, he was as upbeat as a kid on Christmas morning. He smiled and complimented Carole with every word.

That's when we learned something important about the medical world. Many physicians are outstanding and are used by God to bring about miracles. However, like every other profession, it's a customer service business. When my wife and children were the customers, my sole priority was to fight for their survival and peace of mind. I would correct anyone, regardless of their degrees and experience, who didn't live up to the highest standard.

MANY PHYSICIANS ARE OUTSTANDING
AND ARE USED BY GOD TO BRING
ABOUT MIRACLES. HOWEVER, LIKE EVERY
OTHER PROFESSION, IT'S A CUSTOMER
SERVICE BUSINESS.

Carole's six months of chemotherapy went well, though the process took a toll on her. For years, she often asked, "God, why me?" That question would be uttered many more times as our family grew.

The doctors suggested we wait at least five years after chemo to have kids. We soon moved to Texas, and Carole was pregnant within three months of going off the pill.

HERE THEY COME!

"SIR, YOU CAN WAIT HERE. SHE WON'T BE LONG," the receptionist said as she pointed to the clinic's empty waiting room. Carole's ultrasound lasted longer than expected, and my undiagnosed attention deficit disorder was on overdrive. After a while, a woman in scrubs walked out, handed me a picture, and walked away without a word.

It looks like a peanut. I thought of the image in the black-and-white photo. *Or maybe a shrimp.*

Regardless of the shape, I was in love. I stared at the picture and refused to blink. My eyes started to sweat when Carole walked out and sat next to me.

"You all right?" she asked with a smile.

"No," I answered, choking on my words.

At that moment, I received a burst of clarity. The care of that peanut and its mother was my sole job and top priority. I went to work every day for one purpose—to provide for my family. My identity would come from them and our relationship with God, not from how we paid our bills. When people asked, "What do you do?" I laughed and replied, "As little as possible!" and told them about our family.

Carole's OB/GYN had delivered hundreds of babies, and we knew Blaire would be one of her last. The doc planned to take her skills to the new world of Botox®, which in Dallas, Texas, was a license to print money.

Everyone said childbirth was beautiful. They lied. The baby was beautiful, but childbirth was nasty. The garbage bag that hung from the action end of the delivery table said it all. America was made great by generations of fathers sitting in waiting rooms while their wives gave birth; however, that was not an option at this delivery. The woman groaning on the hospital bed called those shots.

With an icepack in hand, I posted next to Carole's head, wiped her forehead, and told her she was beautiful.

"Would you like to cut the cord?" the doctor asked as Blaire came into the world.

"Thanks, but isn't that your job?" I replied with a smile.

The next day, a nurse told us, "We're bringing the crib in here tonight."

"Why?" Carole asked with terror dripping off her forehead.

"You need to practice getting up, feeding, and changing your daughter before we send you home," the nurse explained.

Suddenly, our eight-year fear of parental incompetence roared like a lion. When I put Blaire in a car seat two days later to drive home, I feared for her life.

"She has a little jaundice," our pediatrician said on our first visit. "We could put her in the hospital, or we can send home a portable therapy case for her to sleep in for a few days."

"We haven't killed her yet," I replied. "Let's try the do-it-yourself option."

We set the white suitcase with the blue lamp in front of the fireplace. The protection we put over Blaire's eyes was so cute that we called her "Patches" for a couple of years. I slept on the floor next to my newborn baby in the suitcase every night for a week, and I guarded her like a Doberman.

FOR THREE YEARS, BLAIRE'S SMILE AND LAUGH made her the picture-perfect child. Carole and I developed rudimentary parenting skills, but we knew that lightning rarely struck the same crib twice, and the next one could be more challenging.

"So, Mrs. Boatright, have you been taking fertility drugs?" asked Dr. Doug, Carole's new OB/GYN.

"No, not at all," she replied. His question seemed odd.

"Do twins run in your family?"

"No," she responded again, even more curious than before. "Why do you ask?"

He looked at her and said, "Your blood work came back very high, and based on the size of your uterus, my gut says there may be more than one in there."

This guy must have crashed his Harley without a helmet, she thought. With two-year-old Blaire at home, we planned on having two children at the most.

"You know, I wondered about that," I said that night. "Remember when you took the early pregnancy test before Blaire was born? That second little line was hard to see. When you took the test last week, that line was as dark as night. I thought, *Wouldn't it be funny if it was twins?*"

"Well, we have a 2:30 appointment next Thursday for a sonogram," she replied, her excitement mixed with panic.

Carole tried to relax on the table while the sonographer covered her stomach with jelly. The tech maneuvered the probe around like a beach comber with a metal detector, then stopped.

"Here's one," she said as she circled a small dot on the screen. A few seconds later, "There's number two," and she drew another circle.

When the technician didn't stop the exam, I asked, "What are you doing now?"

"Looking to see if there are any more," she smiled.

"STOP!" I shouted, afraid I might have a heart attack at any moment.

Only two dots were found. A few minutes after the exam, we went to Dr. Doug's office for a consultation.

"We found something unusual," he started. "Your twins are identical, but even with identical twins, there should be a thin membrane separating them in the placenta. We didn't see that membrane on your ultrasound. If it's not there, then one or both may not develop normally or even survive."

"WE FOUND SOMETHING UNUSUAL,"
HE STARTED. "YOUR TWINS ARE IDENTICAL,
BUT EVEN WITH IDENTICAL TWINS,
THERE SHOULD BE A THIN MEMBRANE
SEPARATING THEM IN THE PLACENTA.

Wow, we thought. We grew to love the idea of having twins. Both our mothers suffered miscarriages, so that was a possibility, but we didn't expect this news. The doctor told us to schedule another ultrasound for two weeks later. If the membrane appeared, then everything would be fine. If not, we'd have some serious decisions to make.

Those two weeks seemed like two months. *What would they find, and what would it mean?* During the second ultrasound, our relief was palatable. The membrane appeared, and everything was fine—or so we thought.

Carole's pregnancy with Blaire had been a mother's dream. A little morning sickness and that was it. This one, however, was another story. Carole felt fatigued from the start, and she soon developed gestational diabetes. Her doctor ordered her on bed rest by month five.

"Clay, come in here," Carole called from our bedroom one night during week twenty-six.

"What's up?" I asked as I walked in.

"I have blood spots on my nightgown," she said with a nervous look on her face. After a quick call to the doctor's answering service, we headed to the emergency room.

"One benefit of a high-risk pregnancy is no lines, no waiting," Carole said as they whisked us past the crowd in the ER to an examination room on the maternity floor.

"So, you're having some bleeding?" the nurse asked as she put a belt around Carole's waist. "Let's make sure the heartbeats are okay."

She moved the belt's saucer microphone and stared at the monitor. After a few seconds, she found Baby A and marked the spot on Carole's stomach. She moved the saucer again.

"In addition to yours, I'm hearing only one heartbeat," the nurse said after a couple of minutes. "We're going to call your doctor."

She made the call, came back, and tried again, but still no second heartbeat. For twenty minutes, she found only one. As each minute passed, Carole and I sank deeper into depression. Was our baby gone? What was the condition of the baby she'd found?

Oh, you've got to be kidding, I thought as the door opened and a white coat walked in. The doctor on call that night was a founding member of the obstetrics practice and planned to retire next year. He also had the personality of a brick. A white ghost who looked ninety years old with an Einstein mop for grey hair, he limped into the room at a snail's pace and never acknowledged us.

Dr. Ghost didn't say a word as the nurse gave him an update. When she finished, the old man took his liver-spotted hands and felt Carole's stomach with his 1950's stethoscope. In less than ten seconds, he said, "Put it here."

The nurse placed the microphone where the doctor pointed and smiled. There was Baby B, hiding behind its twin. Carole and I felt the air return to our lungs. The doctor smiled, patted Carole's hand, and left the room. The lesson of the day was to respect and appreciate our elders, who've seen it all.

Four weeks later, Carole sat across from Dr. Doug.

"Well, dear," he said, "Your readings are off the charts. I know you don't want to, but I'm putting you in the big house. You are mine until those kiddos are born."

Carole protested but then saw the bright side. Blaire needed to be potty trained, and my mother flew in to help. If there was ever a time to be out of the house, this was it.

At pregnancy week thirty-three, three weeks into her hospital stay, I walked into Carole's room and stopped in my tracks, astounded at what I saw. My wife looked like a gigantic bell curve. On her back, Carole's stomach must have been four feet higher than her head and feet.

"You are the largest human being I've ever seen!" I exclaimed.

"Come over here, sweetheart," Carole smiled. "I'm going to kill you now."

MY WIFE LOOKED LIKE A GIGANTIC BELL CURVE.
ON HER BACK, CAROLE'S STOMACH MUST
HAVE BEEN FOUR FEET HIGHER THAN
HER HEAD AND FEET.

I was in trouble but obligated to share the truth. The next morning, as I climbed out of the shower, I heard the phone ring.

"Hello?" I answered.

"It's me," said Carole. "Come back to the hospital. I started having contractions last night. We're having babies today!"

"So, which one do we name Mia and which one is Paige?" Carole asked while she was rolling down the hall to the operating room.

We'd picked out their names months ago, but we hadn't decided which twin would get which one.

"Let's flip a coin," I suggested. What better way to determine the most important element of a person's identity than random luck?

"Whoever comes out first gets the name," I said as I pulled a quarter out of my pocket. "We'll go alphabetical. Heads it's Mia; tails it's Paige."

I counted fourteen medical professionals in a delivery room that was the size of an airplane hangar. Two doctors, an anesthesiologist, and a nurse for Carole. Four neonatal nurses were assigned to each twin, with a supervisor to oversee them. The job of some guy in a smock who was hanging out remained a mystery. If someone had brought chips, beers, and a big-screen TV, the party would have been a blast.

Carole's doctor recommended a Caesarean section over traditional childbirth. Carole didn't care; she wanted them out. I stood next to the gas man at her head, behind a screen over her chest to block the view.

Paige came out, and the doctor handed her to the neonatal team. Mia appeared ninety seconds later. Ecstatic, I walked over to hold my baby girls. Both precious gems were perfect, so I turned to tell Carole and share the excitement. That's when I realized I was no longer behind the protective screen. The doctors continued to work on my wife, and I vowed never to eat a rare steak again.

Paige and Mia lived in the NICU for three weeks. They would have been released earlier, but they needed to learn the most basic of human activities—how to eat.

Carole cried every night after the babies came home. "They won't nurse, and I haven't slept since they got here. I can't do it anymore."

"You nursed Blaire for a year. What's different now?" I asked.

"I don't know! They won't eat! Why did God give us twins? I'm not competent to do this!" Carole screamed.

"Maybe you should try a little longer," I suggested.

"What part of 'they won't eat' don't you understand?" Carole replied with a look that could melt rock.

"Okay, okay. Call the pediatrician, and ask him what we should do," I replied, fearing for my life.

"Start them on powdered soy formula," our pediatrician instructed when we called. "If that doesn't work, we'll find something else."

"One can costs $20 and makes two gallons of formula," I calculated in the aisle at Toys "R" Us. "Each child drinks an eight-ounce bottle eight times per day. That's a half gallon per child per day. Double that for twins, and we'll go through a gallon every day. Heck, I may need a new job!"

As though newborn twins weren't crazy enough, that same week, the company I'd joined six months earlier went through a major restructure. One morning, the chief marketing officer called me into his office.

"Clay, everything you see around you is about to disappear," he said. "I'm leaving, and the department is being eliminated. You, however, have a choice. I can negotiate an exit package, or you can take a lateral position in another division. I know those folks pretty well, and I suggest you take the package."

"There could not be a worse time for this conversation," I replied after a long pause. "I brought my newborn twins home from the hospital three days ago. If there was ever a time when

I don't need to be looking for a new job, it's today. I'll take the lateral."

In our first ten years of marriage, Carole and I had lived in four different cities and managed life through cancer, chemotherapy, and a difficult pregnancy. We now had three children under the age of four and faced a possible layoff from a new job. God was fine-tuning our stress management skills, and in a couple of years, we would learn why.

HARSH REALITY
OR GOD'S PLAN?

"**T**HEY NEVER SLEEP!" Carole said in frustration. It was 1:00 a.m., and Carole circled the family room with a screaming Mia in her arms. I heard Paige cry from the nursery and retrieved her to circle the dining room. We soon developed a system where Carole went to bed after dinner, and I stayed up until 2:00 a.m. Carole would be on call until 6:00 a.m. when I got up for work. Four hours of sleep a night was our norm for over ten years.

"MAYBE THIS WILL KILL A FEW MINUTES," Carole said as we walked into the furniture store. Blaire held her mother's hand while I pushed the tandem twin stroller.

"Shopping is something normal families do," I replied, trying to sound positive.

Two minutes later, Mia screamed at the top of her lungs. That triggered Paige, who sat behind her in the stroller, to do the same. Twenty people stared as though we were the most mutant parents in history, unable to control our children. Carole started to cry as we turned and left the store. For years, we only went to church as a family because every other place was too risky.

FOR YEARS, WE ONLY WENT TO CHURCH AS A FAMILY BECAUSE EVERY OTHER PLACE WAS TOO RISKY.

"PLEASE FILL OUT THESE FORMS, and the doctor will be in soon," the pediatric nurse said at our two-year well-baby visit.

"Can walk downstairs while holding hands" and "Uses words like me, I, or you" were two of the twenty-five statements on each form. Carole held Paige and filled it out while I did the same for Mia. When we were finished, we looked at each other, and our stomachs churned. Neither one of us had checked off anything.

"Should we be concerned about this?" Carole asked the doctor with a quiver in her voice.

"There seems to be something going on here," he replied in an unusually nice tone. "I think you should go to Easter Seals for an evaluation. Their director is a friend of mine and will be able to tell us more."

Easter Seals? I thought that was for children in wheelchairs. We didn't know what to make of this. We knew our babies' development was slow, but everyone said it was because they were premature twins and would grow out of it.

Carole sat on the floor of the comfortable office at Easter Seals and held Mia while I tried to get Paige to play with toys. Having happy twins for more than a few minutes was nearly impossible. The director, a developmental pediatrician, watched the girls and jotted notes in her book.

After half an hour, she closed her binder and looked at us.

"I reviewed their charts from your doctor and their evaluations. They are clearly behind their two-year-old peers," she said. "Based on what we're seeing, I think their developmental gap is going to increase."

"What are you talking about?" I replied as my fists tightened. "They're eventually going to catch up. How can you possibly say the gap is going to increase after only one or two meetings?"

"Mr. Boatright, I know exactly how you feel, and it's completely normal. But I've seen thousands of children over the years, and Mia and Paige's development is pretty clear."

"So, what are you saying?" Carole asked as tears formed in her eyes. "What do they have?"

The doctor shifted her weight in the chair. "Well, I hate to diagnose at this early age. Labels can be detrimental to children as they grow, and it really won't affect your course of action."

"That's bull!" I shouted. "You said our children will not develop normally. What do you think is wrong?"

She saw the anger in my eyes and knew she had to shoot straight.

"If I had to make a diagnosis today," she said calmly, as the tension in the room mounted, "I would say they have mental retardation* and probably autism as well."

ELISABETH KUBLER-ROSS, IN HER BOOK *ON DEATH AND DYING*, described the five stages of grief as denial, anger, bargaining, depression, and finally, acceptance. With this bomb dropped in our laps, these described Carole's and my coping process perfectly.

---

*   Note: "Mental retardation" was the medical diagnosis used in 2002. Later, the terminology was improved to "intellectual disabilities."

Denial

"SHE HAS NO IDEA WHAT SHE'S TALKING ABOUT," I told Carole on the way home from Easter Seals.

"I read that she's one of the best, and our pediatrician recommended her," Carole replied.

"He's a quack, too," I responded. "They're premature, identical twins. Everyone knows these types of kids take longer to develop." My attempt to be an amateur neurologist was dismal.

"So what if they can't walk yet?" I continued. "Where do they need to go? No, they can't talk. Big deal! Most people I know talk nonstop but never say anything worthwhile anyway."

"It doesn't seem that bad," Carole said. "Sure, they cry a lot, but they seem aware of what's going on around them."

We shared this unofficial diagnosis with our friends and coworkers. Without exception, we got the same response: "They'll grow out of it." The interesting thing about the denial phase is there are plenty of people to reinforce it.

THE INTERESTING THING ABOUT THE DENIAL PHASE IS THERE ARE PLENTY OF PEOPLE TO REINFORCE IT.

"Let's call our parents and see what they think," I suggested, as though they would have any unique wisdom on this issue. My father had died a few years earlier, and at that moment, I missed him a lot.

Carole's parents tried to be positive and supportive.

"I don't believe it," Carole's mom told us on the phone that night. "There's nothing wrong with those baby girls. They're as sweet as can be, and they'll develop fine. It's going to take time."

"That's ridiculous," was my mom's reaction. "How do you think that happened?"

"I don't know," I replied. "Since they're identical twins with the same DNA, it may be genetic."

"I don't believe it," Mom snapped back. "We don't have anybody like that in our family."

I took a deep breath. "Mom, you don't need to have Uncle Charlie locked in the closet to have a genetic disorder!"

"Well, if that's the reason, then it came from the other side," she said before I hung up the phone.

When we'd told Carole's parents that we were leaving Memphis, Carole and I decided to never make our children feel guilty. Now, after telling my mom about the twins' diagnosis, we decided that we'd love our children equally no matter what.

Anger

"FIRST, I HAD CANCER, AND NOW THIS," Carole often said. She spent a long time in the anger stage.

Since her chemotherapy for Hodgkin's disease, Carole believed that God had singled her out for a life of problems. Now Paige and Mia's challenges convinced her of that more than ever. It wasn't fair. She didn't deserve it, and it made her mad. That belief never went away and would explode two decades later during Carole's ultimate challenge.

I wasn't angry with God, at least not at first. That would come later. Instead, I questioned the medical community. Did something happen during the pregnancy or delivery they never told us about? Did their vaccinations cause this?

"WE KNEW ANNIE HAD DOWN SYNDROME BEFORE SHE WAS BORN," a friend said. "The DS community reached out quickly, and we had people helping from day one," she continued. That was great for them, but families with disabilities that weren't diagnosed for years had to figure it out for themselves.

"It was like a thief in the night," another friend said as she described her son's autism. "He was developing great. Then one day everything stopped, and he lost all his skills."

"We were robbed of our child, and he was robbed of his future," she continued. That feeling was pervasive among autism parents, particularly those whose children had developed traditionally until everything went off the rails. It felt like their hearts were ripped out and never got replaced.

Bargaining

"GOD, IF YOU WILL MAKE MIA AND PAIGE be like other kids, I'll never do anything wrong again."

That prayer sounded pretty good as I knelt by the side of my bed. The problem was that it didn't work when I was eight years old, and it didn't work now.

While Carole felt God was picking on her, I thought He was punishing me. There were a few skeletons in my closet that needed to stay there, and I wondered if my past screw-ups were back to bite me. The Old Testament was full of examples of God's wrath on sinners and their future generations. Moses, one of God's greatest prophets, couldn't enter the Promised Land because he hit a rock with his stick (Numbers 20:8-12). I'd done a lot worse than that.

Years later, God led me to a passage that explained that disabilities were not a punishment from God. John 9:1-3 reads:

> As he went along, he saw a man blind from birth. His disciples asked him, "Rabbi, who sinned, this man or his parents, that he was born blind?" "Neither this man nor his parents sinned," said Jesus, "but this happened so that the work of God might be displayed in him."

We were looking at God from the wrong perspective. The question we should have asked was not, "God, what did we do?" but rather, "God, what do You want us to do now?"

WE WERE LOOKING AT GOD FROM THE WRONG PERSPECTIVE. THE QUESTION WE SHOULD HAVE ASKED WAS NOT, "GOD, WHAT DID WE DO?" BUT RATHER, "GOD, WHAT DO YOU WANT US TO DO NOW?"

Depression

"PAIGE AND MIA ARE GOING TO LIVE WITH US for the rest of our lives," Carole and I said over and over. We first made this prediction when they were four years old. In hindsight, it was premature. However, that pessimistic outlook was hard to escape.

If you search the internet for the definition of *depression*, you'll find over 2.7 million suggestions. The APA Dictionary of Psychology defines it like this: "A negative affective state, ranging from unhappiness and discontent to an extreme feeling of sadness, pessimism, and despondency, that interferes with daily life," and that definition fit our progression through this stage.

Many soldiers have post-traumatic stress disorder (PTSD). Many special needs families go through ongoing traumatic stress disorder (OTSD). "Post" implies a past trauma. Parents of special-needs children, meanwhile, wake up their trauma every morning, assuming their kids slept at all.

Acceptance

This final stage was painful to reach but very fulfilling.

"I guess I have to accept that things will never change," Carole told me one night, frustration obvious on her face. "I should quit trying. They're not getting any better."

"Acceptance is not surrender," I replied. "Surrender means giving up hope, and we're nowhere close to that. The girls are still young, and we have no idea how things will work out. God has a plan for our family. It may not be the plan we want, but He didn't ask our opinion."

Surrendering our responsibilities was not an option, but we had to surrender to God's authority. God was smarter than we were, and we had to get over it.

GOD WAS SMARTER THAN WE WERE,
AND WE HAD TO GET OVER IT.

"So, how've you been?" I asked the young pastor over lunch one day.

"Good," he replied with a little tension in his voice. "I'll be honest. This has been a tough time. The church hasn't grown as fast as I hoped, and the programs I wanted are not in place. I'm pretty stressed."

"That must be frustrating," I said. "Mind if I ask a blunt question?"

"Go right ahead," he said with a smile.

"Those plans you have. Are those your plans or God's plans?" I asked.

"Wow," he answered as he smiled and leaned back in his chair. "That's a great question."

"You know the definition of *stress*?" I continued. "We have our objectives," I put one hand above my head, "and then we

30

have reality." I put my other hand below my chin. "The gap between those two points is what we call stress. The greater the gap, the greater the stress."

The preacher nodded in agreement.

"People spend billions of dollars in therapy to reduce their stress," I told him, "But the math is simple. Lower the gap, and we lower the stress. Most of us think if we bust our humps to raise reality to hit our objectives, the stress will go away. That can happen, but sometimes we need to recalibrate our objectives and move the goal closer to reality."

"I get that," he said with angst in his voice, "but I don't think God wants me to lower my expectations."

"I didn't say *lower,* I said *recalibrate.* Those are two different things. Circumstances have changed, and that's okay. Making an adjustment to fit the new environment is not lowering your standards; it's a sign of maturity. I weigh options based on the situation at the time, then decide. If the situation changes down the road, I reserve the right to improve at any time!" I silently thanked my dad for his advice about not second-guessing our Saint Louis move years earlier.

"That's good stuff," the preacher said. "I needed to hear that. Thank you."

Before Carole and I became parents, I thought the job of being a father was to help our children be more successful than we were. I tried to get the best job possible, move into the right neighborhood, and send them to the right schools. If I set my expectations high, then they'd respond and make me proud.

Then reality hit. The Fatherhood 101 handbook didn't have advice about kids who would never talk and who made strange noises for no apparent reason—for hours on end. Children were supposed to be potty-trained by age three, not twenty-one.

At some point, I took a different approach to fatherhood. Simply put, my expectations didn't matter. God designed and loved Paige and Mia the same as He did Blaire. My job was to help them maximize their God-given potential, whatever that was.

AT SOME POINT, I TOOK A DIFFERENT
APPROACH TO FATHERHOOD. SIMPLY PUT,
MY EXPECTATIONS DIDN'T MATTER.

When I was a young child, my father did not know what I would be like as an adult. His only expectation was that I treat others with respect, and his only hope was that I'd be happy. Those became my goals for my children, regardless of their IQ.

It was, however, easier said than done. I reminded myself there was nothing in the Bible about life being easy, much less fair. It did say that God was smarter than I was, and He chose the family that He wanted me to raise. My job was to trust Him and get it done.

THE MEDICAL COMMUNITY, ROUND 2

"A T THIS AGE, THE DIAGNOSIS DOESN'T MATTER," our pediatrician told us on our first visit after we'd gone to Easter Seals. "It won't change what you do. All parents try to teach their kids how to walk, talk, and eat with utensils, whether or not they have a diagnosis." His son had autism, and this helped calm us down.

Though it may not have mattered, Paige and Mia's first official diagnosis was *pervasive developmental delays, not otherwise specified (PDD-NOS)*. We soon learned this was a catch-all description that doctors and educators used when they did not know what was going on.

A few years later, their diagnosis changed to *intellectual disabilities (ID)*, with a secondary diagnosis of *autism*, exactly what the Easter Seals' director had predicted. Though the two are often confused, they are different. Intellectual disabilities refer to difficulties in reasoning, problem-solving, and other cognitive skills that result in an IQ below seventy. Autism, meanwhile, often involves intense sensory challenges, communication difficulties, problems engaging others, and excessive repetitive behaviors.

"My nephew has autism. It was tough at first, but he's doing great now," someone told us when we shared the twins' diagnoses.

"There's a TV show about a doctor who has autism. You never know how things are going to work out!"

I concluded that comparing our children to other people was one of the worst things we could do. The greatest disservice we do to people with disabilities—or anyone for that matter—is to view them as one homogenous group.

When we told people that the twins had intellectual disabilities, that was usually met with dead silence. Most people didn't know what that meant but were sure it must be bad. It didn't take long to realize the social marketing of one developmental disability succeeded where another had failed. That's when I became *a diagnosis agnostic.* How God brought people to the party and the label we gave it didn't matter. We were all His children, and a few of us needed more help than others.

THE GREATEST DISSERVICE WE DO TO
PEOPLE WITH DISABILITIES—OR ANYONE FOR
THAT MATTER—IS TO VIEW THEM AS ONE
HOMOGENOUS GROUP.

One benefit to an autism diagnosis was that we could get stuff for the twins. For example, in Texas, an autism diagnosis released a host of special education services not available to other students with disabilities. A common joke was, "At one time, parents dreaded getting an autism diagnosis. Now they dread NOT getting an autism diagnosis!"

"I THINK PAIGE HAD A SEIZURE!" Carole shouted through my work phone. "The ambulance is on its way!"

A few days before her fifth birthday, Paige fell to the ground and her eyes fluttered. By the time paramedics arrived, she was resting on her mother. They went to the emergency room, where Paige was evaluated and quickly released.

"It looks like a 7.3 earthquake," I said as I looked at the EEG seismograph readout in the neurologist's office.

"She had five seizures during the thirty-minute test," he said.

"What?" Carole exclaimed. "I was holding her the whole time and didn't see anything."

"They're called *absence* or *petit mal* seizures," the doctor explained. "Paige may have blanked out for a quick second, and you didn't notice it."

We were horrified that Paige might have had seizures for years, and we never knew it. But we were also glad to get a diagnosis for something we could treat.

"This isn't unusual," the neurologist said. "I'm going to prescribe Depakote to treat it."

"I have a question," I said as we prepared to leave. "Since Paige and Mia are identical twins with identical disabilities, should we have Mia tested, too?"

"No," he replied. "She has shown no signs, and we don't schedule EEGs for no reason."

Carole and I talked about it in bed that night and thought it was ridiculous not to test Mia. We called the doctor the next morning and insisted he schedule an EEG.

"Well, you were right, and I was wrong," he said when he called us a couple of days later. "Mia had four seizures during her exam, so I'm sending in a Depakote prescription for her, too."

We thanked him for running the test and for the prescription, said goodbye, and immediately searched for a new neurologist.

"THEY HAVE SOME INTERESTING PHYSICAL CHARACTERISTICS," Dr. Louise, the geneticist, observed on our first visit.

"Really? What do you see?" Carole asked.

"Look at their eyes. They're slightly farther apart than most people, and their fingers are longer too," she replied. "Also, their ears are lower than normal. Most people's ears are centered with their eyes. Paige's and Mia's eyes line up with the top of their ears."

I looked at their faces and saw what she meant. I discovered over the next few weeks that if you stare at strangers' eyes and ears for no reason, they look at you funny.

Despite all the tests, we never discovered why Paige and Mia were born the way they were. This bothered Carole a lot, as each exam that came back normal or inconclusive increased her aggravation. I, on the other hand, didn't care about what or why. I wanted a plan of action. Paige and Mia were born with their disability and were unique because God designed them that way.

PAIGE AND MIA WERE BORN WITH THEIR DISABILITY AND WERE UNIQUE BECAUSE GOD DESIGNED THEM THAT WAY.

"DADDY, CAN I HAVE A PEANUT BUTTER AND JELLY SANDWICH?" six-year-old Blaire asked one Saturday afternoon.

"Of course," I replied, assembling the classic ingredients.

I spread the jelly and peanut butter on the bread and did what master chefs have done for decades—licked the knife. Blaire took her plated cuisine, and I walked into the family room, paused, and gave Paige a kiss on the cheek as I passed by. A few minutes later, I returned and was shocked to see a big red splotch on Paige's face where I'd kissed her. That's how we discovered Paige's peanut allergy and that the slightest transference could cause a reaction.

"Clay, come here!" Carole screamed from the bathroom a few years later. She had the twins in the bathtub while I was laying out their pajamas for bedtime.

"Look at Paige," she said as I walked in. "She has a rash from head to toe! This is so weird. It's like she's having an allergic reaction, but she has had no peanuts."

I knelt next to the bright red child in the tub, and a sharp pain ran through my heart as I realized what had happened.

"Oh my God, I know what it is," I said, afraid Carole would shoot me in the next ten seconds.

That afternoon at work, we'd catered lunch from a Chinese restaurant. When asked if I wanted to take home the leftover Kung Pao chicken, I jumped at the chance to relieve Carole of dinner duties for a night.

"When I boxed up the Kung Pao, I mixed it all together and didn't think about the peanuts on top," I explained, as Carole ran downstairs for some medicine.

"If she has a seizure, you're giving her the EpiPen!" Carole said as she gave Paige a full dose of Benadryl. I prayed I hadn't killed my daughter. Within a few moments, Paige calmed down, fell asleep, and woke up the next morning rash-free.

WHILE THEIR COGNITIVE DISABILITIES WERE SEVERE, Paige and Mia's physical health was pretty strong. When they were pre-teens, we visited their pediatrician, the one who had a son with autism.

"It's tough," Carole told him. "We never know when a meltdown will hit. The constant rocking and turning lights on and off are about to drive me crazy!"

"I'm sorry," the doctor replied. After a long pause, he continued. "You may need to prepare to place them somewhere. In a few years, they will not be cute anymore."

Carole and I went silent. The pediatrician we'd trusted with their care for over a decade was telling us to institutionalize our children. Once again, it was time to find a new doctor.

"WE NEED TO TALK ABOUT IT," Carole said one day when Paige and Mia were around ten years old.

"I don't want to talk about it," I replied.

"We need to evaluate options," she said.

"I don't want to talk about it," I said again.

My father, a World War II, Depression-era member of the Greatest Generation, taught me that there were certain things a man didn't need to know about. A woman's menstrual cycle was one of them.

"There's no way Paige and Mia can understand or manage their cycles," Carole explained. "We have to deal with it, so let's ask around."

Carole was right. We asked doctors about our options for when that day arrived. We learned about different pills, long-term capsules that could be surgically injected into their arms, and devices installed in their abdomens. For a year, what I learned about women's anatomy would have made my father's head explode.

A TV story talked about a woman with cognitive disabilities who'd lived in an institution and became pregnant. Unable to speak, the young woman couldn't tell anyone what happened, but an investigation uncovered that she was raped by one of the facility's employees. That's when it hit me.

"What do you think about hysterectomies?" I asked Carole the next day. "Paige and Mia are women; they can't talk, they don't understand the concept of sex, and will always depend on others. We can't be with them 24/7, and there's a chance that at least one of them will be assaulted someday. If that happens, and she gets pregnant, we can be pro-life all day long, but we're going to have to make an unfathomable decision.

Have our daughter—who doesn't understand pregnancy or childbirth—bring a rape baby to term or pursue an abortion? A hysterectomy eliminates that problem."

"I'm all for it," Carole replied. "They won't get married or have children. If they have a kid, they can't care for it. Besides, when a uterus isn't making babies, all it does is get diseases and cause problems."

Conversations with doctors uncovered something we'd never seen before: generational bias. It seemed like the dividing line was around age fifty. Doctors older than fifty were willing to consider the hysterectomy option, while those younger than fifty thought it barbaric and that it deprived Paige and Mia of their reproductive rights.

"I know this is a sensitive question," Dr. Patricia, our sixty-something-year-old pediatric neurologist, said one day. "Have you decided what you're going to do when their periods start?"

"We've talked to everybody and gotten a hundred suggestions," Carole answered, "but we think hysterectomies are the way to go. I understand it can't be reversed, but there's no scenario under the sun in which Paige and Mia could decide to have children, so what's the point in dealing with periods?"

"Oh, thank goodness," Dr. Pat replied. "I completely agree. To me, it's an obvious solution."

"Who should we talk too?" Carole asked. "Aside from you, it seems like everybody hates the idea."

"It's the younger doctors; I get it," Dr. Pat confirmed our generational suspicions. "I know who you need to see. She's my OB/GYN. In fact, she's known as the doctors' doctor because so many of us go to her. I'll give you a referral."

"I've performed this procedure over a thousand times," Dr. Kathryn told us during our first visit, "but only once on a minor. It was a young woman who had Williams syndrome, and her disabilities were not as severe as Paige and Mia."

41

"Williams syndrome?" I asked. A friend of mine had a daughter with Williams.

"I know you can't tell me the patient's name," I said as Dr. Kathryn nodded her head in agreement, "but was her mother's name Janet?"

Doc froze for a moment, but I could read her face. I knew the family. The father was a doctor. The silence in the room confirmed we were in the right place.

"Performing this procedure on a minor, particularly one who can't give consent, is a big deal," Dr. Kathryn explained. "Our hospital ethics committee needs to approve it, and I'll have to make a case of medical necessity. It's true that women with disabilities are more likely to develop other conditions, so this is a preventative measure."

"Who's the chair of your ethics committee?" I asked.

"Dr. Louise, the head of our genetics department," she replied.

Carole and I laughed out loud.

"Tell Dr. Louise that it's the Boatright twins, and this will sail through," I told her. "She met the girls years ago after they were diagnosed."

Dr. Kathryn called us a week later to share the committee's decision. The procedures were approved faster than she'd ever seen. She suggested we wait a few months after their first periods to do the operations.

IT WAS EASTER MORNING, 2013. We finished breakfast, dressed in our Easter best, and got ready for church. While Blaire walked to the car and Carole finished with Paige, I noticed Mia's pull-up was full and took her to the bathroom as I had a thousand times before.

What the . . . I thought as I sat her on the commode. *Has she hurt herself? Ohhhh!*

"Well, guess what?" I shouted to Carole in the other room. "Mia started!"

"Okay, I'll be right there," Carole answered.

"Don't worry. I've got it," I replied. There was nothing she would do that I couldn't handle. On the way to church, Carole said I deserved the "Daddy of the Month" award. I did not disagree.

"They need to have at least two cycles before we perform the procedure," Dr. Kathryn told us. She scheduled the twins' procedures a month apart in case a complication happened with the first that could be addressed in the second.

Mia went first, and while the operation was a success, the recovery at home was difficult. She was in obvious pain, never wanted to leave the bed, and developed a high fever.

"I've never seen this before," Dr. Kathryn told us when we called. "She should have been down for a couple of days but then bounced back. It sounds like she has an infection of some sort. I'll order some antibiotics and see if that helps."

On Saturday night, a few days later, my cell phone rang. It was Dr. Kathryn.

"I think I figured out what's happening with Mia," she said. "Most women can handle their own toileting after surgery. Mia can't, so the incision is sitting in her soiled pull-up until she's changed. That may be causing the infection."

A month later, Doc Kathryn placed Paige on high-dose antibiotics before her procedure, and the recovery was problem-free.

PAIGE WAS ALWAYS UPBEAT AND HAPPY, and when she turned fifteen, she was a little chubby at 155 pounds. Then, out of nowhere, something happened.

"I don't know what's going on with her," Carole said when I got home one day. "They said she cried at school nonstop and hardly touched her food."

Repeated meltdowns for no reason and refusing to eat became a constant, excruciating cycle for all of us. In nine months, Paige's weight had dropped to eighty-nine pounds, and she would scream for hours as though someone was stabbing her in the heart.

"We've seen her neurologist, talked to dietitians, tried different medicines and diets, yet nothing works," Carole told the gastrointestinal doctor on our first visit. Paige had been tested for everything under the sun, and all the tests had come back normal. Clearly, she was not. Paige was wasting away in front of us, and we couldn't stop it.

"I know this is tough, but I think she needs a g-tube, and quickly," the doctor told us.

Carole and I asked if we could have the office alone for a few minutes to talk about it.

"We're going to have to maintain the line, teach everyone how to clean it, and have special food," Carole said in a panic. "What if she stays on it forever? Her life is already complicated enough as it is!"

I started to say we should do it but then had an epiphany. We needed to put Paige in God's hands. We were watching her die, and the only one who knew why was God. He brought her into this world with her disability and was allowing this mystery to happen. Doctors could not help her, so now it was up to the Great Physician to handle it however He chose.

"We decided not to do the g-tube," I told the doctor when he came back in. I thought he was going to call Child Protective Services on us. He disagreed with our decision but didn't push it.

A month later, Paige's weight climbed back to the upper nineties, but her behaviors worsened, and she became a danger to herself and others. One Saturday, she went totally off the rails, ran around the house, screamed at the top of her lungs, and bit anyone who got near her.

"Take her to the ER," Dr. Pat, the neurologist, told us. "They can calm her down, and we'll try some new medicines on Monday."

Carole stayed home with Mia while I took Paige to the hospital. Her crying and screaming made it a living hell. After two hours in the waiting area, we were taken to an examination room. They took her vitals, then the doctors and nurses disappeared.

"Can someone come in and help us?" I asked at the nurses' station after an hour. "I know you can hear my daughter scream, and she keeps running to the door to leave. Can you at least give her something?"

"No sir, we can't give her anything until she's examined," the nurse replied. "We're trying to get a room on the neurology floor."

My trek to the nurses' station happened three times. On the fourth, six hours after we'd arrived, I took a different approach.

"Here's what's about to happen," I said in a calm but firm tone. "If my daughter doesn't get help in the next five minutes, I'm going to open the door and let her run full speed up and down this hallway wherever she chooses, and you get to deal with it. It's your choice."

A minute later, three uniformed security guards appeared outside our exam room. A few minutes after that, a doctor arrived, and in thirty minutes, Paige got her permanent room upstairs. Helping Paige was more important than the hospital's processes. If I had to throw a human hand grenade—my daughter—into the middle of the ER to get it done, so be it. I never found out if the security team was sent to protect the hospital from Paige or from me.

Four days after Paige was admitted, and after four days of conflicting opinions from at least five doctors, Carole and I called a meeting of the minds.

"There are fourteen white coats, four scrubs, and seven suits in this room," I whispered in Carole's ear as we sat down in the hospital conference room. Our table was in front, as though we were on stage and everyone else was the audience.

"To be candid, we don't know what's wrong," one of the white coats opened the conversation. "We've taped her wrists in cloth to keep her from pulling out the IVs because we need to get nutrients in her. We also need to find the right combination of meds to get her behaviors under control. We can sedate her, but that's not a long-term solution."

"What are your thoughts on medical cannabis?" I asked.

"That's not legal in Texas, so we can't discuss it," was the response.

In one sentence, I changed from being a mild supporter to a passionate supporter of medical marijuana. I had no idea if cannabis would help Paige, but it pissed me off that an option couldn't be considered because of arcane state laws. Paige would never drive a car or put others at risk, yet an addiction to expensive prescriptions was preferred over a plant God Himself invented. It was ridiculous.

"Mr. Boatright, we're going to discharge Paige today," a doctor told me on the phone six days later. I had seen Paige the day before, and nothing had changed.

"Why? She isn't any better. How can you discharge her?" I asked.

"We can't find anything medically wrong with her," was the reply. "We can't keep her indefinitely."

"I guess we have no choice," I said as I picked up my keys.

An hour later, in Paige's room, she wasn't happy waiting for the paperwork to be processed. We went for a walk around the floor to burn off energy. Three minutes and two hallways later, Paige screamed at the top of her lungs and plopped down in the middle of the hall. Nurses and doctors came quickly, but no one could calm her down. Then, as if a light switch had flipped, they decided to keep her. Her timing was perfect, and I was relieved her explosion didn't happen in the car.

"Clay, I've been talking to the medical team," Dr. Pat phoned a week later. "We found a combination of meds that seem to work, and we can send her home tomorrow."

"Great!" I replied, hoping this ordeal would soon be over.

When I called the next morning to confirm pickup, the nurse said, "Mr. Boatright, we need to tell you something. Paige had an allergic reaction last night. She's fine now, but we needed to tell you."

"An allergic reaction to what?" I asked, very confused. "The only thing she's allergic to is peanuts, and that must be in her chart."

"It is. The hospital volunteer who sat with her last night was eating peanut M&M's, and Paige reached out for one. The sitter thought she was being helpful, and she gave Paige an M&M. She broke out in a full-body rash. It scared us to death, but we got Benadryl in her, and she's fine. The volunteer feels horrible about it."

I didn't know what to say.

When I told Carole, she said, "We put a child with a peanut allergy in the hospital to get better, and they gave her peanuts. Of course, they did. Why the hell not? This shit only happens to our kids!"

The hospital's head of nursing and their medical director took me to lunch a few weeks later and apologized. They revised their protocols to ensure a mistake like that would never happen again. They seemed sincere, though the lunch fajitas were probably an effort to avoid a lawsuit.

While our happy and pudgy "old Paige" was gone forever, at least the "new Paige" was stable for the first time in months. Her appetite returned, and her weight came back to a healthier 120 pounds.

WELCOME TO THE BOATRIGHT CIRCUS

"WHAT THE HECK HAPPENED?!" I exclaimed from the recliner as Paige ran downstairs, screaming her head off. It was Saturday afternoon, and she'd been upstairs watching a Disney movie with Mia.

I got up from my chair to calm Paige down when the phone rang. The school district therapist assigned as our in-home trainer was calling to schedule an appointment. She heard Paige scream in the background and asked if it was a bad time to talk.

"Nope," I replied. "It's another great day in paradise!"

Carole walked in and took the phone when we heard the familiar *ding-dong* of the doorbell.

"Good grief!" I exclaimed as Paige and I made our way to the front door. It was a Boy Scout selling popcorn. Since the family across the street had refused to talk to us for eight years because we once failed to buy something from their son, we now bought from every kid who knocked.

"I'll take a kettle corn and a chocolate covered," I said as I reviewed the product list. This was a decade before Venmo, so he needed cash or a check right then. I found Carole, who kept the checkbook, still on the phone with the trainer. She took the boy's order form and closed the door to retrieve her purse.

At that same time, Mia erupted in tears upstairs. With Paige still upset, I left her on the couch and ran to help Mia. As I reached the top of the stairs, I heard the high-pitched *ding, ding, ding* of a door alarm. I looked down in time to see Paige open the front door, scream again, and charge out at full speed past the Boy Scout.

I abandoned Mia in her agony and flew downstairs and out the door to catch Paige before she got to the street. The Scout's mom stood on the sidewalk and gave me a tight little smile. My forced grin said something between *Welcome to our world* and *Write your own damn check and leave us alone!*

I carried Paige back into the house and again closed the door on the scout. By now, he probably thought he'd rung the doorbell of hell. Carole came out of the bedroom with the phone still on her ear, opened the door, and gave a check to the scout, who turned and ran for his life.

THANKSGIVING WAS A FEW DAYS AWAY, and you could feel the holiday spirit revving up. The kids were off from school and excited about Christmas, Santa Claus, and family feasts around the dining room table. Dad enjoyed time off from work, and Mom was proud to create yet another fun holiday for those she loved. That's how holidays were for other families—but not ours. Boatright holidays sucked.

Carole and I fantasized about the Norman Rockwell holiday experience, but it happened only in our minds. Norman never painted a mother frustrated on Christmas as her pre-teen twins threw food across the table, their opened gifts ignored once again—a waste of time and money.

CAROLE AND I FANTASIZED ABOUT
THE NORMAN ROCKWELL HOLIDAY EXPERIENCE,
BUT IT HAPPENED ONLY IN OUR MINDS.

Landlocked in the house for weeks while school was closed, we looked for anything to keep Paige and Mia occupied. A successful holiday had them in the bathtub for hours as they poured water from old Tupperware over and over in a weird sense of hypnotic calm. Facebook antagonized us with pictures of normal families on the slopes in Aspen or on the beaches of Maui, while ours was spent soaking up water that splashed out of the tub.

"School is what keeps me sane," Carole would say. School was a place for both education and government-funded respite. We had no family nearby to help, so a holiday break for us was impossible.

One year, we learned about a holiday respite program for families with disabilities. The brochure read *Guests need to be able to take care of their personal needs with little to no assistance and should not have any aggressive behavior toward other guests.* I laughed out loud and told Carole, "That's not a respite program. That's a monastery!"

The Plano, Texas, park system had a therapeutic recreation program that met one Friday night a month at a local church.

"We've heard lots of good things about this," we said to Addie, the program director, on our first night to leave the twins.

"We're so glad you're here!" Addie replied. "It can be a little traumatic for parents the first time, but Paige and Mia will do great. You're more than welcome to watch through the window if it makes you feel better."

Carole looked at me in fear that I'd screw up our night out.

"That's very kind," I told Addie with a smile. "But if we had those concerns, we wouldn't be here having this lovely conversation. We're not the least bit worried. Trust me, you'll be calling us long before we'll call you!"

They didn't call, and that became our standard for competence. Unless there was significant blood loss, an organization that served people with disabilities needed to handle the challenges rather than call the parents whenever something went off-script.

"I SAW AN ORGANIZATION CALLED HEROES," I told Carole after attending a disability expo one October. "They have weeklong camps during the summer."

"They won't take Paige and Mia," she replied. "Everybody wants them to be potty-trained and tranquil. If they could do that, we wouldn't need a camp!"

"They said they take kids like ours," I continued. "It's run by special ed teachers, so they know the drill. Let's see what happens."

The sign-up a few months later felt like a race for free Rolling Stones tickets. Registration went online at midnight, and all 150 slots were gone by 12:05 a.m. Slow birds got no worms.

"Today we go bowling, then putt-putt tomorrow, and yoga on Wednesday," said Kim, one of the leaders, when we dropped off the twins on Monday.

"Yoga?" I laughed. "Well, that should be interesting!"

"You'd be surprised," Kim replied. "Kids will do things here that they would never do at home."

The HEROES summer camp turned out to be a great experience for all of us, and when they added camps for winter and spring break, we knew God was looking out for us. A disability program that took our twins was an indescribable blessing because most discriminated against those with severe needs.

A DISABILITY PROGRAM THAT TOOK
OUR TWINS WAS AN INDESCRIBABLE BLESSING
BECAUSE MOST DISCRIMINATED AGAINST
THOSE WITH SEVERE NEEDS.

We found one mainstream program that wasn't afraid of a challenge. The thirty-minute dance class on Saturday mornings was great for five-year-old Mia and Paige. Sally, the studio owner, believed that all kids should enjoy the arts, and their instructor, Mandi, had a nephew with Down syndrome. That year's spring recital featured close to a hundred traditional students ages four to forty-four, plus Paige and Mia, the only two members of Mandi's special needs class.

We were 90 percent sure that Paige and Mia wouldn't perform when we left Friday night's practice. They grabbed my neck when we arrived and cried as soon as we approached the stage. The lights were bright and the music loud. Mia and I played outside while Paige sat with eight-year-old Blaire in the dark auditorium to watch the practice. Carole was heartbroken.

Mandi suggested we arrive early for the Saturday afternoon dress rehearsal to let them play on stage without the music and lights. Mia and Paige ran around and sat quietly in the wings stage right with the other kids. However, when Mandi and Shelby (her teenage assistant) tried to lead them onstage, they wouldn't move. At least they'd made it farther than the night before.

Carole and I were the only parents backstage when the show started on Saturday night. While we waited with the twins, a little girl walked over and asked, "Why don't they talk?"

"They're learning, and they will," I replied. They would speak when God was ready.

"I'm so proud of you!" I told them when it was time for their dance. Mandi came off stage, looked at me, and I nodded for her to try. She and Shelby led the twins in front of 250 people with the lights bright and "Twinkle, Twinkle, Little Star" on the speakers. With their instructors holding their hands, they did their little twirls, circled their marks, and exited stage left to rousing applause. They performed perfectly.

Carole and I ran across backstage as the four came off. When we arrived, Mandi had a tear on her cheek. She told us some of the teenage and adult dancers were crying offstage as well. My eyes sweated when Mandi gave Paige and Mia roses and star medals for their success.

SIX-YEAR-OLD PAIGE HAD TAKEN ANTIBIOTICS for about a week. Lethargic and listless, Mia ignored her all day. Paige went to bed early one night, and after a few minutes, Carole and I noticed Mia was missing. I went upstairs to search.

Paige and Mia slept in the same twin beds my siblings and I had used decades earlier. Though sleeping in the same room, Paige and Mia never got in bed together, as each demanded their own space. I was certain the last time they slept together was in the womb.

Once upstairs, I noticed the overhead light was on in their room. That was odd because it was turned off when I left. Paige lay awake on her bed by the wall, quietly holding her pillow. Meanwhile, Mia sat at Paige's feet as though she was guarding her sister. To make it weirder, when she saw me, Mia squawked like Captain Jack's monkey in *Pirates of the Caribbean*.

I flipped off the light switch, which inspired Mia to climb to her knees, turn it back on, then slide back to her post. Back in her position at Paige's feet, Mia gave a quiet smile that said, *You can leave now. I have it under control.* Mia knew her sister was sick, and she was going to help. I left them in peace.

"LET'S GO TO COTTON PATCH FOR DINNER," Carole suggested one afternoon. We tried to eat out at least once a week to give Carole a break and to help our ten-year-old twins develop restaurant skills.

Chicken strips for Paige and Mia, hamburger for Blaire, and country-fried steaks for Carole and me. It didn't get much better than that! Blaire was a methodical eater, completing one thing on her plate before moving to the next. Paige's and Mia's eating strategies were more sinister. Before chowing down on their meals, they first stole food off the plates around them. Their logic was simple: If they ate their meals with everyone else, there might not be food left to steal later. However, clandestine procurement of fries or chips up front was a win. When it came to food, *what's mine is mine, and what's yours is mine* was their modus operandi.

Dinner was uneventful, as the fun was saved for the end. One of Mia's nuances was her refusal to leave the dinner table at home or anywhere else. She didn't fight to stay; she simply wouldn't move. How a seventy-pound little girl with minimal muscle control could become a marble statue anchored in her chair was both impressive and aggravating.

Carole took Blaire and Paige to the minivan while I spent five minutes trying to coax our youngest, to no avail. Serious manhandling was required. I pushed all the dishes and glasses to the far side of the table and tried to pull her legs out of the booth. This sumo wrestling took another three minutes to get her on her feet. With my hands on her shoulders, we moved at a snail's pace through the maze of tables and patrons.

The door was in sight when Mia petted the back of a nice man eating his dinner with his family as we walked by. He glanced at me with a startled look. I smiled and said, "She gets this way when she drinks. I'm sorry."

Half a step further, Mia spotted rolls on the family's table and *wham* her hand went into the breadbasket. The table shook like an earthquake, and five water glasses jumped in the air. Once again, I apologized for the thief.

"Oh, no problem," the man replied, while his wife and children grabbed their plates like precious jewels.

Two servers held the doors wide while we slithered out. With Mia chomping on her ill-gotten biscuits, I shouted for the restaurant to hear, "She has a twin sister, too!"

"I SAW YOU IN THE PARKING LOT and set this table for you," the server at Steak 'n Shake said as we walked in the door on a Saturday night.

"Wow, that's impressive," Carole replied. We protected the other guests as we walked to our table.

"Let me get something out here fast. Would they like French fries?" asked the server, Melanie.

"A plate of lemons would be great," Carole replied, refer-ring to the twins' favorite snack. "So, do you have a sixth sense for spotting crazy families when they walk in?"

"No," Mel laughed. "I noticed your girls as they got out of the car. I have a son with autism."

We struck up an immediate friendship. For a year, we went to Steak 'n Shake every Saturday night. Mel would even set our table before we arrived.

"I'm exhausted," Mel shared one night. "Between work, school, and motherhood, there are not enough hours in the day."

"What are you majoring in?" I asked.

"Special education," she replied. "I always wanted to be a teacher, but school isn't cheap, and I need to cover the tuition bill this week."

"How much is it?" I inquired.

"One seventy-five," she answered.

We finished our meal, and I walked up to the counter. The clerk ran my credit card; I wrote in the tip and handed it back.

She tried to process it, but the system beeped in error. She tried again, and it beeped again. Bewildered, she retrieved her manager.

"Are you sure about this?" Carlos, the manager, asked as he took control of the machine. "The system can't handle a tip over $100, so I'll need to split the bill in two to make it happen. This is very kind."

"We special needs parents need to stick together!" I told him. Neither Carlos nor I realized that he would become a special needs dad himself in a few years when he and Mel got married.

"WE SPECIAL NEEDS PARENTS NEED TO STICK TOGETHER!" I TOLD HIM.

"GO OUT WITH FRIENDS?" Carole laughed when someone asked about our social calendar. "We don't have friends; we're a special needs family!"

That wasn't totally true. We knew some people at church, Carole enjoyed time with moms from Blaire's school, and I ate lunch with my coworkers. Friends to enjoy on weekends or travel, however, were not in the mix.

"Who's that on the floor with Paige?" I asked Carole when I got home one afternoon. The twins had been working with their in-home therapist when Angela came by to retrieve her daughter from an afternoon spent with Blaire. She met Paige for the first time and immediately sat down to become part of her world. Now that was class.

Angela and her family attended Prestonwood church too and would join us for dinner after church on Saturday night, often at Tin Star, a nearby Tex-Mex restaurant. This became a highlight of our week.

When the nine of us walked in, we operated like Seal Team Six, each one with a specific job and position. Angela's family would get to the restaurant first, find a place to sit, and get chips on the table before we arrived. Waiting for food was not our children's strong suit. The adults got Paige and Mia seated. I ordered food, and during dinner the traditional kids were on point for retrieving refills. It worked in harmony and enabled our family to engage with one from the "normal world," which rarely happened.

"I NEED YOU TO COME HOME. My dad's not doing well," Carole said when she called me at work. Her parents had moved to Plano in an apartment nearby, and a home healthcare nurse came in a few days a week. Now and then, they spent the night with us. That morning Richard woke up with chest pain, and Carole called the paramedics.

The place was a madhouse when I got home. Besides the five of us who lived there, there were Carole's parents, their home health nurse, six paramedics and firefighters, plus an ambulance and firetruck parked out front. I walked in and sat next to the twins on the couch to keep them out of the way.

The paramedics wheeled Richard to the ambulance for a night's stay in the hospital. Carole and her mom followed in our car.

"What's so funny?" I asked my in-law's nurse when everyone left. She laughed and smiled from ear-to-ear.

"One of the firefighters asked if this was a nursing home or a halfway house," she replied. "When I told him, 'No,' he said, 'Well, between the old couple in one room, two disabled kids on the couch, and you in your scrubs, we weren't sure.'"

I laughed and said, "Ya know, if it looks like a duck and quacks like a duck! I wonder which category they put me in!"

"You will not believe what our witch neighbor has done now," Carole said as she stormed into the house, using another word that rhymes with witch. Because our neighbor refused to share the cost of repairing our mutual fence a year earlier, Carole couldn't stand her.

"She just posted a *No Trespassing, Keep Out* sign on the property line pointed straight at us!" Carole exclaimed, madder than a wet cat.

"Why would she do that?" I asked.

"Yesterday, the air conditioner repair guy parked in front of our house," Carole explained, "so the school bus dropped Paige and Mia in front of hers. The grass was dry, so we walked across her yard to get to our door."

I walked out and saw the sign halfway between our house and the sidewalk. Now pissed as well, I thought, *What's the Christian way to handle this?* and had an idea.

I went to the garage, returned with our own sign, and placed it a few inches from the neighbor's billboard. It looked like a TV ad for a boxing match, a red *No Trespassing, Keep Out* facing off against a white "He Is Risen" Easter cross. The symbol of our risen Lord used in a neighborhood dispute may not have been the classiest thing to do, but it seemed right at the time.

The next morning our neighbor turned her sign more toward the street. The showdown got her attention. Later that day, the HOA president knocked on our door with the trespassing sign in hand. He had driven by, realized what was happening, and offered to throw hers away if we took ours down. Six months away from Easter, we agreed, and the world went back to normal.

It had been a long day, and the tension in the house ran high. Mia and Paige would not go to bed and were having meltdowns. Carole was exhausted and retreated to our bedroom.

"Daddy, am I going to have to take care of Paige and Mia when you and Mom are gone?" asked ten-year-old Blaire as I tucked her into bed. Her question caught me off guard. I realized that whatever came out of my mouth next would have a lasting impact on Blaire and how she viewed her sisters. I paused to gather my thoughts.

"No," I replied. She looked at me to explain.

"You know how you get bothered that I go to so many meetings that involve Paige and Mia and not you?"

She nodded yes.

"Your friends' parents can help with your activities, and Mom and I appreciate it so much," I explained. "There's no one to do that for Paige and Mia. I must do it for them because no one else will.

"We want to create a world where Paige and Mia can live on their own, and you won't have to take care of them. As your father, I'd love for you to be part of their lives. However, that will be your decision to make, not mine."

> "WE WANT TO CREATE A WORLD WHERE PAIGE
> AND MIA CAN LIVE ON THEIR OWN, AND YOU
> WON'T HAVE TO TAKE CARE OF THEM."

Blaire gave me a hug as I pulled up her covers. I was not going to tell a ten-year-old that her destiny was to endure the challenges she saw her parents experience every day. Though they could frustrate her, Blaire adored her sisters and was their biggest fan. I believe eliminating the fear of the future had a positive impact on their relationship.

"When you're dead, you're no longer part of the equation," I often told parents planning for the future. Many envisioned the siblings caring for their brother or sister after the parents died. While that may have been great for some, every family and disability was unique.

Taking care of someone who could speak, had passive behavior, and could handle their own personal hygiene was very different than caring for someone who has none of those skills. Just because a sibling was raised in the same house didn't mean that he or she naturally had the best caregiving abilities, plus they had hopes and dreams of their own to pursue. A parent's belief they could legislate from the grave was a pipe dream.

"BLAIRE, THIS IS OUR LOCKBOX where we keep our passports, birth certificates, and other important information." Inside was an envelope with *Paige & Mia Important Information and Key Contacts* written on the outside.

"In case Mom and I die together in a car accident," I continued cheerfully, "There's a letter listing who you are to call, in order, along with their contact information. It includes your aunt Marta, our lawyer, financial planner, and people who manage the support services for Paige and Mia. They have our complete trust and will give you good advice on what to do."

WHILE BLAIRE LOVED HER FAMILY, she was also a typical teenager.

"Two and a half years," Blaire said as we pulled the car into our neighborhood.

"To what?" I asked.

"In two and a half years, I won't have to do what you tell me anymore," she said, roughly six months shy of her sixteenth birthday.

I paused to decide if I should laugh or verbally jump on her. A third option came to mind.

"You're right," I told her. "In two and a half years, you won't have to do what I tell you, but you know what's really cool about that law? That same law says in two and a half years, I don't need to give you a place to live, feed you, pay for your education, or put clothes on your back. What do you think about that?"

Flashing her million-dollar smile, Blaire turned to me and said, "I love you, Daddy!"

"I know you do! I never doubted that for one minute!" I replied as we laughed it off.

CAROLE AND I HAD SEPARATED household management responsibilities when she decided to stay home with Blaire. She paid the bills, cooked, and handled insurance and home improvements. I oversaw car maintenance, cleaning the kitchen after dinner, kid duty until 2:00 a.m., and earning money. This worked for fifteen years, and we rarely discussed our respective jobs.

"I think I want to change careers," I told Carole one night.

"Since I have no idea what you do now, go ahead," she replied. "Make the same amount of money and have good health insurance is all I ask. What do you want to do?"

"Special needs parents are under a lot of stress," I replied. Carole nodded in agreement. "You and I manage it pretty well, and I think I can help others. Maybe I should become a licensed professional counselor."

That idea received the same look as when I mentioned buying an above-ground hot tub. Patronizing skepticism.

"If that's what you want to do, go ahead," she offered in support. "I have this image of someone sharing their darkest pain and you say, 'Oh, get over yourself and grow the hell up!'"

I laughed because I could see that too!

Amberton University offered an LPC degree program nearby. Over the next few semesters, I learned about systems theory and insights from Carl Jung, Sigmund Freud, Alfred Adler, and B. F. Skinner.

"If I want to be an LPC to help people, maybe we should go to one to see what it's like," I told Carole one day. She agreed it wouldn't hurt, and we made an appointment with a practice that was sponsored by our church. Mark, our counselor, was a former pastor who'd decided to change careers as well. After three sessions, he wanted to meet with Carole and me separately.

My one-hour appointment opened with me providing a twenty-minute monologue on everything Mark needed to know. I shared all my strengths, weaknesses, vices, and relationship details regarding my parents and wife. I was intimate with my problems, knew their root causes, and why I had, or had not, dealt with them. Mark listened to my verbal diarrhea and offered his thoughts.

"Clay, I've been doing this for twenty years, and you are by far the most self-aware person I've ever met. You know your issues, are not afraid to own them, and know what to do about them. I honestly don't know what to tell you."

"I'm not sure if that's a compliment, but I'll take it as one," I laughed. "I also know why. Unlike 99 percent of Americans, I don't believe my own bullshit."

Mark smiled as I continued.

"Most people create the image they want others to see and overlook who they really are. I'm too lazy to concoct a fake facade and then work to become it. Our days have too much real crap to deal with."

Mark nodded as though he understood but may not have agreed. A few months after our sessions, I stopped taking the LPC classes because of my work schedule. My dream of being a counselor had gone the way of the hot tubs.

SCHOOL DAYS

"I RECOMMEND THE TWINS GET IN PPCD," our pediatrician told us. Preschool Program for Children with Disabilities was administered through the school system for children with learning challenges. We had paid out of pocket for Applied Behavior Analysis (ABA) therapy, which didn't work, and we were happy to try something new. Carole was excited to have the house to herself for a few hours each day.

"Our first step," said the parent liaison at Beaty Early Childhood School, "is to have an ARD meeting."

"An ARD meeting. What the heck is that?" we asked. The admission, review, and dismissal meeting included parents, teachers, and school administrators to design the child's IEP, or individualized education program. At three years old, Paige and Mia had entered the alphabet soup of abbreviations and acronyms known as *hell*.

Millions of people had become amateur doctors by using WebMD, so I decided to become a disability expert in the same way. Internet forums were my classroom, and there was one consistent theme. "You can't trust the schools. They always cut corners."

Julie, Paige and Mia's first teacher, was an unbridled bundle of energy, while the principal, Susie, exuded pure style and sophistication. We didn't have teachers and principals like that in 1970s Memphis. Linda, a special education advocate who was recommended on the forums, joined us for the first ARD.

"Carole and I are new to this, and you know a lot more than we do." I opened the meeting with the obvious. "We've asked Linda to advise us, but Carole and I will make the final decisions for Paige and Mia."

If they'd given medals for arrogance and obnoxiousness, I'd have won gold.

"We all want the best for Paige and Mia," Susie replied, "and we're always open to new ideas. If there are things we can do better, let's go for it!"

Wrightslaw, the well-known guide for special ed parents, had never reported a principal who said that. We thought this was supposed to be a combat zone. For the next ten years, we brought the peacekeeping donuts to these four-hour marathons.

Two years of PPCD led to the first day of elementary school.

"My babies are coming to my school!" third-grader Blaire shouted with excitement as we drove everyone to Haun Elementary. Blaire ran to her class while two paraprofessional aides took Paige and Mia to theirs.

I had two epiphanies as Carole and I walked back to the car. First, the people best trained to teach Paige and Mia were found in the public school system. Emergency rooms and public schools were the only enterprises in the United States legally required to take everyone who came in the front door, and ERs could transfer their patients out once they were stable. Public schools had to keep them for the long haul, and for this parent of twins who were usually rejected because of their disability, that was huge.

"This train's going to stop someday," was my second aha. The twins would spend over fifty years as adults out of school, much longer than the thirteen or so they would spend in it. As the father responsible for their long-term care, I needed to understand the adult support system long before they needed it. My realization was a gift from God because most parents waited until their kids were teenagers before they tried to figure that out.

AS THE FATHER RESPONSIBLE FOR THEIR
LONG-TERM CARE, I NEEDED TO UNDERSTAND
THE ADULT SUPPORT SYSTEM LONG
BEFORE THEY NEEDED IT.

"I'D LIKE TO CALL AN ARD MEETING for Mia and Paige next week," said Kathleen, the principal at Haun. "There's a new program you should hear about that may benefit the girls." We were less than halfway through the school year.

The twins' teacher sat at the head of the table, followed by Kathleen, Carole, then me. On my other side sat a young woman who looked like a student. We assumed she was a college intern earning practicum hours for graduation.

"The twins are doing fine," Kathleen opened, "but the district has started a new program called an Experiential Learning Classroom that we think would be perfect for them. It's onsite at Saigling Elementary."

"Hang on a minute," I said in defense. "Are you dropping the twins? Why can't they get what they need here?" The professional advocates had said that each school was required to provide the accommodations their students needed, and I was ready to fight. Dammit, we forgot to bring donuts.

"Clay, let's talk about the program. If you don't want to pursue it, we'll do the best we can for them here. I give you my word." That was a powerful promise for a principal to say out loud. Out of respect, we listened to their sales pitch.

"Hi, my name is Christina. I'm the ELC team leader at Saigling," said the young woman next to me, apparently not a student. She shared that the program would have two teachers and two aides for seven students, including Paige and Mia. That four-to-seven ratio was much better than the three-to-sixteen at Haun.

"Kathleen," I asked when Christina finished, "What would you do if they were your children?"

Without taking a breath, she replied, "I'd put them at Saigling. Try it out, and if you don't like it, bring them back here, and we'll do what we can."

"Saigling and Haun start school at the same time," Carole pointed out. "How can I bring Blaire here and take the twins to Saigling at the same time?"

"A bus will pick up the twins, and if Blaire is ever late, we won't count it," Kathleen replied. They'd packaged this pitch well.

Carole and I looked at each other and had a silent conversation. Throughout our marriage, we always agreed on the big-ticket decisions, which meant that I did what she wanted.

"Young lady," I said to Christina with a touch of arrogance, "Your workload is about to increase by 40 percent—a very active 40 percent. Can you handle it?"

That twenty-something-year-old teacher looked me dead in the eye and replied with the confidence of someone thirty years older. "Yes, we can, and I want your children in my class."

In almost six years of meltdowns, bites to the bone, intense stress, sleepless nights, and constant rejection, no one had ever said that they wanted our twins.

A tear rolled down my cheek, causing Christina's eyes to sweat as well. That's when I realized the most powerful statement someone could say to a special needs parent was, "I want your child."

Christina, her co-teacher Kristin, and a variety of para-professionals were our teaching partners at Saigling for six and a half years. Half-day ARD parties gave us new perspectives because of Kellie, the school principal. In the Plano Independent School District, the sun rose and set on the principals, the CEOs of their schools. If frustrated parents wanted the central office to overturn a school decision, they wouldn't get far. Nothing happened on a school campus that the principal did not approve. As a result, I wanted a close relationship with all of Paige's and Mia's school leaders.

. . . THE MOST POWERFUL STATEMENT SOMEONE COULD SAY TO A SPECIAL NEEDS PARENT WAS, "I WANT YOUR CHILD."

"This makes no sense," I said during a third-grade ARD meeting. "Every school district in North Texas has special ed kids progressing faster with iPads. Meanwhile, Plano refuses to use them. Why?"

"I don't understand it either," the principal replied, "but it probably has to do with cost. We need a parent to push it forward, and if you'll do it, I'll support you." She knew I enjoyed a good fight.

The district's head of technology was very polite. He knew why I made the appointment and answered my questions before I asked them.

"We use Dynavox," he said, as the first reason for avoiding iPads. The Dynavox was a bulky communication device that screamed, *I have a disability!* iPads, meanwhile, were everywhere and used by everybody, including siblings and parents. Many special ed students loved iPads but refused to touch the significantly more expensive Dynavox.

"We don't support Apple technology," he continued with excuse two. That wasn't true because senior high CAD/CAM classes used full-sized Macs every day.

"If we give iPads to special ed students, then we need to give them to all students." Excuse three made no sense either. If that were the case, then all students would have a Dynavox.

"You may be able to afford it, but not all parents can," he replied when I offered to pay for the twins' tablets. "Plus, we don't allow privately owned devices to use the school Wi-Fi." By that time, my thirty minutes were up, and I wanted to escape.

I called a friend on the school board to vent. She said that instead of requesting iPads for everyone who needed it, I should offer the twins as a test case. I could buy the devices, and the school could select the software. The school jumped on the idea, ran it up the hierarchy, and soon Paige and Mia became among the first of Plano ISD's 50,000 students to use iPads in the classroom.

"CLAY, YOU SHOULD RUN FOR THE SCHOOL BOARD," our trustee friend said a year later. "It would be good to have your special ed perspective on the board. You would do well." I thought about it and picked up an election packet a week later.

Holy crap, this thing goes on forever! I thought that evening. There were forms to fill out, a thorough explanation of the election process, and expectations of a trustee. I attended board meetings and candidate forums to understand the commitment, but that night I realized the time it would take for me to do it right.

"We need to talk," I told Carole as I walked into our bedroom after midnight. My desire for late-night conversations, particularly when she was falling asleep, had driven her crazy for years.

"This board trustee thing will take a lot of time away from you and the girls. Before we move forward, are you okay with that?"

"Let me ask you this," she said as she rolled toward me in the dark. "If you're a board trustee, you're supposed to care about all students in Plano, right?"

"Of course," I replied.

"So, here's my question. Do you really care about all students? I know you care about our kids and the others in special ed, but do you give a flying rat's ass about the valedictorians going to Harvard?"

I thought about that for a minute and threw the packet away the next morning.

THE MOVE FROM ELEMENTARY TO MIDDLE SCHOOL felt like driving off a cliff. It didn't seem that different for Blaire, but middle school was a shock for the twins. The days of fun were over, and education got serious.

We already knew the principal at Robinson Middle School from Blaire's time there. Carole and I met with her a few days before school started.

"It's hard to explain to someone who doesn't have a special needs child," Carole opened up. "My day is total chaos, and I never know what's going to happen."

"You never have time to rest," Billie Jean replied, "between school, doctor visits, therapies, running the house, and keeping him in line." She laughed as she pointed at me. We appreciated her empathy.

The special ed section included several rooms along a dedicated hall. We were a little concerned about segregation from the traditional students, and the cooldown room caught our attention. Smaller than a closet, the door had been removed and the walls covered in blue rubber. It was literally a padded room.

"I don't like this," I told Shannon, the twins' new lead teacher. A member of our church, Shannon was the district's curriculum specialist for years, and she knew Paige and Mia.

"They had a cooldown room at Saigling," Shannon pointed out.

"It was a lot bigger and had a bean bag chair," I replied.

"Clay, it's a place for kids who are overstimulated to calm down for a minute or two, and an adult is always with them. If you want, we'll bring in a bean bag!" Her confidence, smile, and love for the twins reassured us.

"Will you let us know if they're ever in here?" I asked.

"Absolutely. In fact, we're legally required to tell you," she replied. In three years at Robinson, the twins never needed the cooldown room.

"I'm testifying before the Senate Education Committee next week," I mentioned to the principal one day. "It's on a controversial topic—cameras in the classroom. I think they're a great idea, but a lot of educators are against them. What do you think?"

"I'm in favor of them," she replied to my surprise. "Not only do they protect the students, but they also protect the teachers. If a parent claims their child came home with a bruise and accuses the teacher, it would be great to pull the tape to see what really happened. Everybody wins." Once again, she proved that Robinson was the right place for our girls.

School had one major stressor, however. To be technically correct, it was a person. Carole and I called her Nurse Ratched, named after the nurse from hell in the movie *One Flew Over the Cuckoo's Nest*. Carole would go into a rage whenever Nurse Ratched called and told her one of the twins had a slight fever.

If Blaire was sick and the school called us, we knew it was important. What no one admitted is that every day, thousands of regular ed students had diarrhea at school and nobody knew. However, for a special ed student who needed help in the restroom, a case of the runs set alarms off across the building.

Nurse Ratched used her thermometer like a weapon, and her target was my wife.

"Hi Carole, I need you to come pick up Paige. She has a fever," Ratched would say.

"How high is it?" Carole asked.

"One hundred point two," Ratched replied.

"That's not a fever. Why did you take her temperature?" Carole's own temperature would rise.

"Well, she wasn't acting like herself. She seemed listless, so we took her temperature. You need to come get her."

There was no doubt that at least a hundred kids showed up at school that day acting listless, and twenty of them had a temperature. Nobody was sticking glass tubes down their throats to check the heat, but Nurse Ratched couldn't wait to do it on the special ed kids.

"I'm not coming," Carole would tell her. She wasn't going to take it anymore. "The bus will be there in a couple of hours. Send her home like normal."

If a nurse randomly took Paige's temperature, it was their problem, not ours. If Paige had thrown up or had gotten injured, that would be different, but a periodic temperature check was not enough to warrant a trip home.

"We need to talk about Mia," Shannon told us in her office prior to an annual ARD. "She continues to put her hands in her pants, and it's becoming a problem. We try redirecting and focusing her attention, but it's not working."

"Does she need to go to the bathroom, or does she have a rash that she's scratching?" I asked.

"Uh, no," Shannon replied, looking straight at Carole.

"So, what do you think it might be?" I asked, bewildered.

"Clay, she's becoming a woman and is discovering her body," Shannon said.

I processed that for a moment. "Oh no, no, no, no, no, no, no. Are you saying she's playing, uh, stimulating herself?" I asked in complete denial.

"It's totally natural but also inappropriate in the classroom. We think if she wore a bodysuit under her clothes, that would prevent her from reaching down there."

Shannon had been down this road before, and we agreed with her. This was a great reminder that even though someone had autism and couldn't talk, their bodies were still working like they were supposed to. Darn it.

The further Paige and Mia advanced in school, the less we engaged. Life skills versus communication and academics were the priority. Nonetheless, every day brought a different adventure.

"Hello, Mr. Boatright. This is the principal at Plano Senior High," the voice said through the phone. We had met once before, but I couldn't recall her name.

"Let me start off by saying that everything's fine," she continued. When someone started off with that, you could guarantee it wasn't going to be fine.

"Uh, oh. What happened?" I asked.

"We had an incident today," she continued. "During a class change, Paige left her room, ran out into the main hall, and started taking her clothes off."

Of course, she did, I thought to myself.

"The hall was packed with students when Paige sat down and started to remove her clothes," the principal explained. "Her teacher couldn't get her to stand up, so he grabbed her by the ankles and dragged her back to the classroom. It was an inappropriate way to get her back in, but he had to get her out of the hall. The last thing we want is to have a cell phone video of Paige stripping in the hallway pop up on the internet."

"I totally agree," I told her. Sometimes drastic situations call for drastic action, protocols be damned.

"DADDY, ARE YOU OKAY?" Blaire asked as we sat in the auditorium for twenty-two-year-old Paige and Mia's high school graduation. Blaire saw a tear roll down my cheek.

"I'm good," I sniffled. "For eighteen years, school was a safe place with programs to help them grow. Now that's over, and it's scary."

"What happens when the school bus stops coming?" was a question that was asked by every special needs parent. We were better prepared than other families, and I thanked God for that Friday Night Revelation almost twenty years earlier.

NO MISTAKES

"MOM, WHERE DID MY NAME COME FROM?" I asked my mother around age eight. "Is anybody else in the family named Clay?"

"No," she replied. "When they wheeled me into the delivery room with you, a Bible verse came to me. It was the passage where Jesus spat on the ground, formed the clay, and placed it on the eyes of the blind man. That's why we named you Clay."

It meant little to me at the time, and that conversation moved into my subconscious memory.

ONE FRIDAY NIGHT IN LATE 2004 was extremely rough. Paige and Mia screamed, Blaire was upset, and Carole cried, which almost never happened. Meanwhile, I did what any good father-leader would do: I retreated to the bedroom. I couldn't find a solution to help my family, and I was mad at God.

"God, why did You do this to Paige and Mia?" I prayed before falling asleep. "And why did You do this to me?" That question was on my mind as I drifted off.

I rarely went to sleep angry, but when I did, I'd wake up the next morning hotter than the night before. My emotions seemed to marinate overnight. However, things were different that Saturday morning. It was like waking up outside on a bright spring day with a cool, refreshing breeze blowing over me.

To help people like Paige and Mia was my first conscious thought, which I immediately interpreted as helping people with severe disabilities.

I lay on the bed in complete silence. Given the peace and tranquility of that moment, there was no doubt that the Holy Spirit had visited me in the night and answered my question. It had to be the work of God because, given my mental state and life priorities at that time, there's no way I would have created that answer on my own. That was my Friday Night Revelation.

Now what do I do? I asked myself. Immediate action had to be taken, so I did what millions of people did every day in search of answers—I Googled it! I sat down at the computer and typed four words, using the vernacular of the time: "mental retardation Dallas help." The first link to pop up on the screen was for an organization I'd never heard of called The Arc of Dallas.

I looked at their website and called them on Monday.

"We're looking for new board members," Erin, the development director, said after explaining the organization and its services.

A week later, I met the board president, executive director, and a few members of the staff. They were an impressive organization, and I joined their board the next day. The Holy Spirit said Paige and Mia had disabilities to help others like them, and this seemed like a good place to start.

Not long after my Friday Night Revelation, Carole and I attended a worship service at Stonebriar Community Church, where Pastor Chuck Swindoll offered a sermon on special needs families. He described John 9:1-3:

As he went along, he saw a man blind from birth. His disciples asked him, "Rabbi, who sinned, this man or his parents, that he was born blind?"

"Neither this man nor his parents sinned," said Jesus, "but this happened so that the work of God might be displayed in him."

The last line jumped out. First, disabilities weren't a punishment from God. Many people—and some faiths—believed that those born with a disability were victims of God's wrath, but this passage proved otherwise.

Second, "this happened so" was a reminder that key elements in our lives are often planned by God for a specific purpose, and He doesn't make mistakes. These were not random accidents but elements that God used to paint His ultimate portrait.

Third, the power of God can be manifested in each one of us, regardless of our capabilities. Nowhere does the Bible say that God uses only those with a certain IQ or stature. In fact, the opposite is true. Noah and Jonah were not worldly scholars. The disciples and other followers of Christ were a ragtag group of sinners, frequently dismissed in their day. God, however, used these men and women to change the world.

. . . THE POWER OF GOD CAN BE MANIFESTED
IN EACH ONE OF US, REGARDLESS OF
OUR CAPABILITIES.

A few weeks after discovering John 9:3, I memorized it. The New International Version was my go-to Bible, but that day I pulled out the Revised Standard, the version my mother had used. With each word committed to memory, my eyes drifted from verse three to verse six.

A cold chill ran down my back. The hairs on my neck stood on end, and I lost my breath. Verse six in the Revised Standard reads: "As (Jesus) said this, he spat on the ground and made clay of the spittle and anointed the man's eyes with the clay…"

The conversation with my mother about my name flooded back. It was no coincidence that a Bible passage that came to my mother forty years earlier would resurface this way. God had a plan for the Boatrights, and at that moment, my life changed forever.

INTO ACTION

I WAS AN AISLE MAN. Easy access to the airplane's bathroom was not important, but I liked spilling a leg or elbow out in the aisle, winning a little more space than others in my row. Passengers packed the late afternoon flight from Las Vegas to Dallas, and American Airlines assigned me a window seat. I wasn't excited, but at least it averted the hell of all placements— a middle seat.

Checking email on my phone as the other passengers boarded, a loud voice caught my attention. I looked up and saw a man in the aisle ahead of me having a heated conversation with the flight attendant.

"This is my seat," he asserted as he pointed to the man in 12C.

"I'm sorry, sir, but that's not what's on your boarding pass," the flight attendant replied.

"Listen, I'm on this airline fifty weeks a year, and my travel agent always books the aisle. I checked online this morning, and this is my seat!"

"Sir, I don't know what to tell you, but his boarding pass says 12C. Yours says 13B," she calmly explained and pointed to the empty seat next to me.

As steam rose from his ears, he made a comment about deserving better treatment. Despite his protest, Mr. Privileged begrudgingly scooted down the row and plopped next to me. Oh yay, this was exactly how I wanted to end my day.

For three and a half hours, we said nothing to each other. I played games on my phone and stared out the window, looking forward to getting home and a good night's rest.

The pilot came on the public address system as we approached Dallas and announced that we were in a holding pattern but would be on the ground soon. The collective groan from the cabin almost drowned out the "Oh great" from my seatmate. Neither of us wanted to stay on that plane, but at that moment, there seemed to be a strange sense of camaraderie in our mutual desire for the trip to end.

It was twilight toward the west, and the ground was now visible. For some reason, after over three hours of dead silence, I said to 13B, "It's amazing how brown the ground is. Hopefully, we'll get some rain soon."

Not expecting a response, I was shocked when he replied, "Yeah, I know. My yard is looking pretty rough."

Wow, he can speak and not get pissed, I thought to myself. We had time to kill, so I asked where he lived. He said Dallas, and we started irrelevant small talk. It soon became apparent, however, that this conversation was very relevant.

"What do you do?" asked Jack. (Yes, 13B had a name.)

"I work in the food business, but most people know me from my disability advocacy. I have three daughters, and my identical twins have severe intellectual disabilities and autism."

Jack went dead silent.

"I may need your help," he said after a few moments. "My daughter has Down syndrome and is about to age out of school. We're trying to find options for her, but it's tough, particularly getting help from the state."

"Jack," I replied with a chuckle under my breath, "Have you heard of The Arc of Texas? It's the state's oldest nonprofit that helps people with developmental disabilities."

"Sure, I get some of their emails."

"Well, I'm their board president," I said. The surprise on Jack's face was obvious.

For twenty minutes, we talked about adult day programs, group homes, and government support programs as we circled DFW Airport and pulled up to the gate. Jack took copious notes with every word.

"Clay, now I know why God put me in this seat," Jack said as we unbuckled our seatbelts. "Thank you."

I thought the same thing, humbled to be used in God's plan at thirty thousand feet.

My revelation about God's purpose for Paige and Mia's disabilities changed my life forever. Until that moment, I'd been confused, mad, and frustrated with conflicting priorities. God spelled out my purpose and initiated a series of events I never could have planned.

GOD SPELLED OUT MY PURPOSE
AND INITIATED A SERIES OF EVENTS I
NEVER COULD HAVE PLANNED.

My education started at The Arc of Dallas. As part of a fifty-year-old national network of advocacy organizations, it offered a variety of programs for adults and children with disabilities. It also understood their daily lives. Sherry, The Arc's executive director, took this enthusiastic new board member under her wing. Though I was not the first parent inspired to save the world, I took a different approach. Job one was not to solve them but to learn. Knowledge flowed in daily, and I soaked it up like a sponge.

"Parkland Hospital called again," I overheard in The Arc office one afternoon.

The call was from the emergency room. Eighty-five-year-old mom passed away and was lying on a gurney, while fifty-year-old Jimmy was in the waiting room and had no idea what was going on. A call like that came in every couple of months.

"That's going to be us one day," Carole said. "Paige and Mia are going to live with us forever, then we'll die of old age, and nobody will know what to do."

"That won't happen," I replied, determined to avoid a life-sucks conversation. "Paige and Mia will stay at home as long as it makes sense, then they'll move out. Why should Blaire be the only one to enjoy getting away from us!"

"Clay, do you see those ladies over there?" Sherry asked when I walked into The Arc's annual Christmas gala. The DJ cranked up the Pointer Sisters, while two hundred people hit the dance floor for the time of their lives.

"They're from the Junior League, and I need you to do your Clay thing!" she continued as I laughed. The "Clay thing" was explaining the unique challenges families with disabilities faced in very simple terms, sometimes inspiring a laugh and a tear along the way.

"We made a presentation to them last week about sponsoring events," Sherry explained. "One of them said, and I'm quoting, 'Our members may not feel comfortable working with your clients.' Once I processed that she said that out loud,

I invited them to come tonight and see our clients in action. I need you to make them feel at home."

"Got it!" I said as I made my way over to the Louis Vuitton Blondes, four of Dallas's finest. In addition to their sparkling bling, they were wearing smiles—a good sign.

"Hello, ladies, I'm Clay, President of The Arc. Thank you so much for coming. We really appreciate it. Are you enjoying yourselves?"

"Oh Clay, yes, we are! This is so much fun," one of them replied. "We didn't know what to expect. Everyone is smiling and laughing and having a marvelous time. It's great!"

"I'm glad you're enjoying it. If you have any questions, please let me know," I said and walked away. They'd anticipated a bunch of sad people in wheelchairs drooling in their soup with harp music in the background. Our victory was not living down to their expectations.

The number of people with disabilities continued to outgrow available services, and the media took notice. They would contact The Arc for quotes and families to feature in stories, and the staff often referred them to our family. Pretty soon, Carole, the cute, middle-class mom and her adorable twins, popped up in articles and television stories at least once every six months.

THE NUMBER OF PEOPLE WITH DISABILITIES
CONTINUED TO OUTGROW AVAILABLE SERVICES,
AND THE MEDIA TOOK NOTICE.

Our family's notoriety led to friendships with several reporters who I'd contact with different ideas. An episode of *Law & Order* one night stirred feelings like my Friday Night Revelation. At 2:00 a.m., I finished writing an article, and I reached out to my contacts at the *Dallas Morning News*. The article ran the following week and was picked up by newspapers from Georgia to Alaska. A few years later, the newspaper gave permission for the article to be used in a college textbook on the psychology of suffering. It was titled "Ignoring God's Children."

> *It's startling to see your life depicted on a television show, especially when that show is a top-rated crime drama. This week's episode of* Law & Order, *titled "Challenged," showcased the challenges facing millions of American families, including mine.*
>
> *The plot revolved around Pete, a 47-year-old man with intellectual disabilities who had been sent to a state institution by his parents when he was only three. Willowbrook, the real-life New York institution that closed in 1987, was described as a "hellhole." Now living in a community home, Pete today enjoyed his unique group of friends, diverse caregivers, and the respect of his employer.*
>
> *This episode's moral dilemma questioned parents who willingly place a child with disabilities in a state institution. It bitterly, and quite accurately, described the immeasurable stress that disabilities bring to a family and the lack of support they receive.*
>
> *The writers, however, made one mistake. Several times the dialogue referenced, "That's how things were done then," suggesting times have changed. For many families, things have hardly changed at all.*
>
> *As the parents of 8-year-old identical twins with severe developmental disabilities, my wife and I have come face to face with this moral dilemma. Our pediatrician recently told us that we should "prepare to place them somewhere" in the next couple of years. In other words, he recommended we institutionalize our children.*
>
> *This happened in 2008, not 1964. While many parents make this difficult decision, it does not come easy. As reported in the* Dallas Morning News, *all eleven Texas "state schools" for people with developmental disabilities are currently under investigation by the Department of Justice for alleged abuse.*

Most families want to stay together. However, as shown on Law & Order, the physical, emotional, and financial strain on a family without support can be insurmountable. Community-based services cost less than institutionalization, but Texas people with disabilities endure waiting lists for nearly a decade before receiving help. Not surprisingly, for families who can no longer go it alone, there is no waiting required to place their child into our DOJ-investigated institutions.

With almost 100,000 people on waiting lists and more citizens institutionalized than in any other state, Texas ranks among the worst five states in the nation for disability services. Collin County has the lowest per capita funding for people with developmental disabilities in Texas. In cruel irony, Plano was recently named the wealthiest city in the United States.

In other words, the most prosperous city in America is at the bottom of the bottom for helping God's children most in need.

The lack of adequate care for people with disabilities is pervasive. Earlier this week, local news aired video from a Dallas County school bus showing a driver choking a student with disabilities. While most professional caregivers are compassionate, abuse is not isolated to certain areas, just as it was not isolated to the 1960s.

Caring for people is a matter of choice. Our state lawmakers can choose to end the waiting lists, while the federal government can choose to provide funds to upgrade education, housing, and employment options. Our schools can choose to improve staff training and provide quality programs and supports. Our churches can choose to respond to God's word and "treat with special honor" those he created differently.

While these choices are not cheap, the costs pale in comparison to the destruction of families who have no choice at all.

—Clay Boatright, Dallas Morning News Editorial, November 15, 2008.

POLITICS. There was an insidious relationship between elected officials and the disability community. Politicians controlled funding for social services and education while creating regulations that impacted most aspects of a disabled person's life. Despite the connection, many politicians didn't consider people with disabilities as constituents but rather costs to be minimized. Thus, the need for advocates.

"Hi, my name is Clay Boatright. I live in Plano, Texas, and my wife and I have three daughters, including identical twins with severe developmental disabilities." That line opened hundreds of conversations and legislative testimonies. In one sentence, from a white man in a suit, they learned my name, marital status, that I valued all my children, and why we needed to chat. To get a Texas politician's attention, I leveraged my privileges with a smile.

... MANY POLITICIANS DIDN'T CONSIDER PEOPLE
WITH DISABILITIES AS CONSTITUENTS
BUT RATHER COSTS TO BE MINIMIZED.

"There are almost no day programs for adults with disabilities in Plano," I shared with two city councilmen early on. When we reviewed statistics about the number of people in our area with disabilities, one councilman asked, "Are those people really disabled or simply lazy and don't want to work?" Ninety seconds into the meeting and I already wanted to scream.

"HI, I HAVE TWO CHILDREN IN SPECIAL ED," was how I greeted a school board trustee after a meeting.

"Oh, special ed, you'll want to talk to Mary (another trustee). She has a daughter in special ed." His response implied special needs parents were an elite private club who talked only to each other. If I was black, would he have shuffled me off to their black board member?

"MEDICAID, ISN'T THAT FOR ILLEGALS?" asked a state representative.

Oh, dear God, I thought to myself.

Funded by both federal and state governments, Medicaid was the lifeblood of the disability community, funding virtually all medical and daily living services. Billions of tax dollars for those unable to care for themselves, 60 percent went to people with disabilities and the elderly, and 30 percent to nondisabled children. It was one of the largest line items in the state budget. Legislators determined the funding, and this goofball was clueless about a billion-dollar topic he was elected to manage.

"I'M SORRY, THE SENATOR SENDS HIS REGRETS, but he won't be able to join us today," said the twenty-two-year-old junior deputy assistant for Constituent Affairs in a conference room of the Hart Senate Office Building in Washington, DC. Intelligent and ambitious, like 90 percent of Congressional aides in Washington, she could also have been a model for *Vogue*.

"Where is he?" I asked, looking at the disappointed faces of the rest of our group. The meeting had been scheduled for months, and we traveled from Texas to DC specifically to meet with our senator.

I voted for this guy, so get his happy ass in here! I thought in the back of my mind but kept to myself.

"A group from the Down Syndrome Society is touring the Capitol today, and he went over to say hello. However, I can take your information and make sure he sees it," the junior deputy replied with a smile.

"Let me make sure I've got this straight," I responded, mustering up as much indignation as possible. "The senator has time for a photo-op with kids who have Down syndrome but doesn't have time to discuss the supports and services many of them will need as adults. Am I hearing that right?"

She cleared her throat and repositioned the notepad on the table, clearly wanting to be someplace else. That was okay because people learn a lot in uncomfortable situations.

TEXAS POLITICIANS WERE EASY TO UNDERSTAND. Most of them loved to help children, as long as it didn't cost anything. Banning certain books from school libraries or mandating who used which bathroom could generate a lot of "family values" political passion because they didn't affect the state budget.

The most controversial political topic of our time was also budget free. However, if a saved fetus became a child with a disability and required long-term care the family could not afford, those same child-protecting politicians disappeared in the wind. For them, pro-life ended when the umbilical cord was cut. After that, child and mom were on their own.

Frustrating conversations were not limited to elected officials. They also permeated those overseen by politicians and government bureaucrats. Our school district's after-school program discriminated against students with disabilities due to requirements that made it impossible for them to participate. During a meeting with the district director of special education, she said, "Every student went somewhere after school today, so it must not be a problem."

From her standpoint, if families weren't participating, they must not have wanted it, regardless of the reason. That was like saying if a person with no teeth can't eat steak, then he must not be hungry.

"WHY ARE AUTISM PARENTS ALWAYS MAD?" asked a senior health administrator in Austin. Surprised by the bluntness, that one took me a second.

"It's not anger; it's frustration," I replied. "The aggressive behavior of some kids with autism makes it different from other diagnoses. Most programs are designed to support people who don't have those challenges, which makes finding help for kids on the spectrum almost impossible." My response was total improv but also true.

DISABILITY ADVOCACY WAS, FOR ME, like golf was for many others. Most of the time, it was maddening, but hitting a great shot occasionally kept me coming back. A passionate Independent, I engaged Republican and Democrat officials with equal vigor for one simple reason. Disabilities didn't discriminate based on political party affiliation, so neither did I.

"The county has a fund to support housing development," Collin County Judge Keith Self, a member of my brother's graduating class at West Point, told me over lunch. Elevated home prices in our area were a major obstacle to creating group homes for people with disabilities.

Over the next few months, I coordinated two county agencies, a nonprofit organization, and a for-profit service provider to create a proposal for the county commissioners to consider. As a result, they awarded $50,000 in seed money to create more group homes. This was a great example of advocacy raising political awareness and the elected leaders responding in kind.

DISABILITY ADVOCACY WAS, FOR ME, LIKE GOLF WAS FOR MANY OTHERS. MOST OF THE TIME, IT WAS MADDENING, BUT HITTING A GREAT SHOT OCCASIONALLY KEPT ME COMING BACK.

"FLORENCE SHAPIRO AND I are meeting next week, and I'm a little nervous," I told Joe, a pastor at my church. Shapiro was my state senator, and this was one of my first meetings with an elected official.

"I know Florence. It will be fine," he replied. "If it gets awkward, offer to pray for her."

"Really?" I said with surprise. "You don't think that would be weird? I think she's Jewish."

"I'm pretty sure she knows she's Jewish," Joe laughed. "Give it a shot."

The meeting with Senator Shapiro and her district liaison went well. As we wrapped up, I remembered Joe's advice and asked, "Senator, would you mind if I said a quick prayer?"

"By all means. Thank you!" she replied with a smile and a surprised look on her face. We bowed our heads, and I thanked God for the senator, the district liaison, their service, and their time.

"Nobody's ever done that before," her aide said quietly as we walked out of the room. From then on, I offered to pray at every one-on-one meeting I had with a politician. Not once did anyone object.

Senator Shapiro, a Republican, chaired the Texas Senate Education Committee. After our conversation in her office, whenever I testified before her committee in Austin, she acknowledged me from the dais with a personal comment. This elevated my credibility with other committee members.

I OFFERED TO PRAY AT EVERY ONE-ON-ONE
MEETING I HAD WITH A POLITICIAN.

One time, another senator's aide whispered to me, "Mr. Boatright, Senator Davis would like you to join a meeting in Austin next week" during a Senate Education Committee hearing. Senator Wendy Davis, an eventual Democratic nominee for governor, served on the committee as well. She'd heard my testimony one day and asked for help to solve a constituent problem. I flew back to Austin the next week, honored that a well-known senator whom I'd never met wanted my perspective.

"CLAY, DIFFERENT ADVOCACY GROUPS have conflicting opinions on the same issues," Representative Jeff Leach, a member of my church, said on the phone. "I'd like for you to pick a team of advocates you trust and develop a list of key priorities for the next legislative session."

Eight fellow advocates and I created a wish list of initiatives for the legislator to consider when he went back to Austin.

Several months later, Representative Leach invited me to a meeting in his Capitol office with the new executive commissioner of Health & Human Services in Texas. Toward the end of the meeting, Leach said to the commissioner, "Clay knows this well. You should hire him at the agency!"

I didn't know whether to be flattered or terrified.

SENATOR LETICIA VAN DE PUTTE, a powerful member of the legislature and a future candidate for lieutenant governor, hurried down the back hall of the Capitol with her arms loaded with books. I saw her from a distance, and as a shameless opportunist, I pounced.

"Hello, Senator Van de Putte. My name is Clay Boatright. I've testified before your committees," I said when I caught up to her.

"Of course, I know you," she replied with a smile as she put out her hand. "You're the superdad."

I almost fainted.

With one statement, Senator Van de Putte validated my advocacy and affirmed several of my beliefs. Disability-related meetings were dominated by professional advocates, providers, and bureaucrats who were all paid to be there. It was nice to know that elected leaders recognized those of us who did it for free because there weren't very many. In addition, when it came to children's issues, mother advocates were omnipresent, while fathers were so rare it caught people's attention.

"OF COURSE, I KNOW YOU" . . . "YOU'RE THE SUPERDAD."

TAMELA, A CONSTITUENT OF Representative Rodney Anderson and mother of a daughter with autism, walked down to the speaker's table in the House hearing room. She was nervous during this first visit to the Capitol and wasn't comfortable speaking in public. When it came time to give testimony about her daughter, she froze. The room sat dead silent and everyone, including the legislators, felt uncomfortable.

Representative Anderson sat on the dais with his peers. When the room went quiet, he poured a glass of water, walked down from the platform, and handed it to Tamela. He took one step back and stood by her side while she regained her composure. Anderson provided the quiet support and encouragement Tamela needed to talk about the most important person in her life.

"Okay, that's pretty darn cool," I said to a long-time legislative advocate sitting next to me.

"I've been here ten years, and I've never seen anything like that," she replied.

"WE'RE HERE WITH COUNTY COMMISSIONER Kathy Ward about her plan to boost nonprofit investment in Collin County," said the radio host during my long drive home from work.

Hey, I live in Collin County and do nonprofit stuff! What's up? I thought to myself.

As I listened to Ward share her idea, it was clear that she was someone I needed to know. That evening, I went on the County Commission website, found her email address, and sent her a note. Five minutes later, she replied and asked if she could drop by the house that Saturday afternoon.

Wow, I thought, *an elected official is coming to meet us, not the other way around. Is that even legal?*

Carole was sitting in the backyard, watching the twins play in the hot tub, when the doorbell rang. I answered the door to a sensory overload of Texas-sized blonde hair and a Sarah Palin button pinned on a bright white T-shirt that screamed *Vote for Kathy!*

What the heck has landed on our doorstep?! ran through my mind.

"Hi, I'm Kathy. Are you Clay?" she shouted with a huge smile on her face. I thanked her for coming, and we walked through the house to the backyard. Campaign season was underway, and she was block walking, so I assumed we'd chit-chat for a few minutes, and she would leave. We had church in an hour, so the timing worked well.

"Commissioner Ward, this is my wife Carole, and those are our twins, Paige and Mia," I said, motioning to the girls twelve feet away. She shook Carole's hand and complimented our home, then did something that floored us. The commissioner walked over to the twins, sat on the edge of the hot tub, and struck up a conversation with our eight-year-old daughters—two people I had told her could not speak!

"Hi, Paige and Mia. My name's Kathy. It's great to meet you," she said as her focus moved from us to them. "Where do you go to school? Do you like it? I used to be a special ed teacher at Plano East."

Carole and I looked at each other in amazement.

This elected official sat on the edge of our pool for two and a half hours. She played with the twins, discussed disability issues, and displayed empathy for families we'd never seen from a politician. In addition to teaching special ed, she also coached the drill team, Blaire's extracurricular passion. We skipped church that night and gave birth to a permanent friendship.

"You gotta teach 'em when they're young" is good advice for many things, including political advocacy. A forum for first-time candidates in an upcoming Republican primary was a good venue to meet and greet. The electorate in Collin County ran deep red, so victory in the Republican primary meant winning the office.

"Hey Clay, I'm so glad you came," my new friend Commissioner Kathy said when I arrived. "Here, I want you to meet someone," she continued, pulling me by the arm across the room.

"Clay, this is Van Taylor. He's a candidate for state representative. Van, meet Clay. He and his wife have three beautiful daughters, and he's very knowledgeable about disability issues," she said as she walked away.

Mr. Taylor and I sized each other up and exchanged small talk. He was a businessman and a former Marine, and he learned that this amateur advocate worked in the food business.

"A lot of people with disabilities need state support to survive," I shared. "Is that something you might be interested in?"

"I haven't given it much thought," he replied. That was fair, considering I hadn't given it any thought until the twins' diagnoses.

Saturday afternoon, a few weeks later, was cold and rainy when I pulled into the parking lot of an elementary school for early voting. The two cars in the lot, I assumed, belonged to the poll workers. As I walked to the building, out of the corner of my eye, I saw someone a hundred feet away, huddled under an umbrella, in the middle of a patch of campaign signs.

Why would anyone be out in this crappy weather all alone? I asked myself and walked over to investigate. I soon recognized the man in a full suit and tie.

"Van?" I asked. "I'm Clay. We met a few weeks ago at the Angelika Theater."

"Sure, I remember. It's nice to see you again," Van Taylor said as I shook his hand.

"Why in the world are you out here alone in a cold rain? You're going to catch pneumonia!"

"It's part of the job," he replied. "You have to get out, meet the people, and ask for their vote."

"We're the only people within twenty miles!" I laughed and exaggerated. Anyone driven to stand alone in the freezing rain to earn my vote was going to get it.

After the election, representative-elect Taylor and I had an official meeting at Starbucks. My PowerPoint presentation covered the most important issues he needed to know regarding families with disabilities. He listened closely.

Taylor eventually moved from being a state representative to a state senator to a congressman in Washington, DC. Along the way, he earned a reputation in the disability community as a man who families could reach out to for help. His staff learned the minutia of disability support and plowed through the bureaucracy on behalf of his constituents.

Yep, you gotta teach 'em when they're young.

"EVERYONE WAS REPORTING ON ME GOING TO CHURCH. It was like *a Democrat in church!*" said the guy on television one night in 2006.

The audience laughed while Jay Leno interviewed a senator from Illinois, some dude named Barack Obama, who'd visited Rick Warren's Saddleback Church the day before. Warren's best-selling book, *The Purpose Driven Life,* was one of my favorites, so I watched the interview closely.

"See that guy?" I asked Carole when she walked into the room. "He's going to be the first Black president of the United States."

A newspaper article the next year mentioned that an information session about Obama was planned in Dallas a few nights later. I'd never attended anything like that before, but after thinking about the Leno interview, I dropped by.

The white guy from Plano was easy to spot in the room of seventy-five. Between the speaker and eavesdropping on nearby conversations, the discussions seemed less pro-Obama and more anti-Hillary. It also became clear that "information session" and "fundraiser" were the same thing.

He probably won't win the nomination next year, much less the presidency, I thought, *but he's a player down the road. I'll give him a couple of bucks.* For the very first time, I pulled out my wallet and made a political contribution.

"I donated to his campaign," I told Carole when I got home.

"How much?" she asked.

"Five hundred dollars," I replied.

"Well damn!" she exclaimed. "I hope he wins."

David, an Obama campaign volunteer, called the next day to say thanks for the contribution. He said the senator would be in town for a major fundraising lunch in a couple of months and asked if I wanted to attend.

"Sure," I replied. "Sign me up."

What started as seventy-five people in a small room a few months earlier now blossomed into a ballroom of a couple thousand. David invited me to join him and his wife at their table near the stage. The guest of honor arrived after everyone finished their tasteless chicken. The crowd erupted in loud applause while the Secret Service cleared a path to the stage.

When Obama finished his speech, he walked off the stage and made his way through the crowd with Ron Kirk, the former mayor of Dallas, by his side.

"Go stand over there!" David pointed to a spot between the stage and the door. "You might be able to shake his hand!"

The idea of chasing celebrities felt icky, but David's enthusiasm was hard to ignore.

"Okay, fine. I'll go stand over there." Less than a minute later, I was face-to-face with Elvis himself.

"Hello, Senator. My name is Clay Boatright. It's nice to meet you." I said as the future president walked up.

"Hello, Clay. It's nice to meet you as well. What do you do?" he asked.

The temptation to say "as little as possible" was huge.

"I work for the Dean Foods Company and do a lot of disability advocacy. My wife and I have three daughters, and our younger twins have severe intellectual disabilities and autism."

"That's great. Raising kids with disabilities takes a lot of patience," he replied. "I'm familiar with Dean. My wife Michelle's law firm did some work for them in Chicago."

"Small world. I hope your visit goes well," I said as he moved down the line.

The next day, an email from David had a photo attached. It showed Obama and me looking straight at each other with our mouths open, as though in a polite argument, with Mayor Kirk in the background picking his nose. For the next decade, I milked that picture like a dairy farm.

A few months later, the Obama for America website had a page focused on disability-related issues and a list of key initiatives. The website for John McCain, Obama's opponent in the upcoming election, had nothing. That's when the trouble started.

Internet sleuthing yielded the email address of a senior member of the Obama campaign. I sent a quick introduction and offered to help, which he forwarded to another staffer.

"Hello, Clay. I'm Kareem Dale, National Disability Director for the Obama for America campaign," read the email. The campaign developed a national volunteer network to reach the disability community and share their plan. As it turned out, they didn't have anyone in Texas—until then.

"You're a Democrat!" laughed a friend at church. "How'd they let you in here?" referring to our politically conservative mega-church.

"No, I'm not," I replied with fake indignation. "I'm a hard-core Independent, proudly bi-political. My vote swings both ways!"

With rampant disdain for political partisanship, my loyalty was to Jesus, family, country, and that was it. When it came to politics, I voted for candidates who were empathetic to people and families with disabilities.

MY CELL PHONE RANG ON NEW YEAR'S DAY, 2009.

"Hello, Mr. Boatright. I'm with the Presidential Inauguration Committee, and we would like to invite you and a guest to the inauguration on January 20. You'll have to pay your own expenses, but you'll receive passes to various inaugural events that week if you choose."

"What? How did this happen?" my sister-in-law exclaimed when told the news.

"Beats me. I'm in the middle of it, and I don't understand!" I replied.

With the inauguration less than three weeks away, we couldn't find anyone to watch the twins, so Carole stayed home. Eleven-year-old Blaire joined me for what would be the kickoff of our annual daddy-daughter trips. Concerts with U2 and Stevie Wonder, Demi Lovato, and the Jonas Brothers led up to the big day. We stood shoulder-to-shoulder with thousands of people for hours, waiting to pass through security. We ran onto the grounds of the Capitol moments before Obama took the oath of office.

THE AMERICANS WITH DISABILITIES ACT, or ADA, is landmark legislation that prohibits discrimination against people with disabilities in all areas of public life, including jobs, schools, and every place open to the public. Signed by President George Bush on July 26, 1990, it was the civil rights linchpin for people with disabilities and is the model followed by other countries around the world.

The summertime heat on the South Lawn of the White House in July 2010 felt like a restaurant oven, particularly to those wearing a full suit and tie. To honor the twentieth anniversary of the ADA, the White House hosted an event and invited dignitaries, celebrities, disability advocates, and one goofy dad from Texas.

The National Summit on Disability Policy coincided with the ADA anniversary, so I stayed in Washington for a few days to become smarter. During the summit's evening gala, I noticed a group of people in a corner with a man I'd never met but had spoken with and emailed several times.

"Hi, Kareem, I'm Clay Boatright," I said when I walked up. "We worked together on the campaign. I'm the dad from Texas."

"Hello, Clay!" He smiled and put out his hand. "It's nice to finally meet you." Kareem was now the special assistant to the President for Disability Policy.

"Likewise. It's great to meet you as well." I replied. "Thank you for the invitation to the inauguration and all the activities this week. I appreciate it. If I can be of help in the future, please let me know." We chatted for another second before I walked away.

Two months later, my cell phone rang. The caller ID said *Unknown.*

"Hello, Mr. Boatright, my name is Jones, and I'm a lawyer with the White House," was his opening line.

Oh crap, what did I do? I thought in a panic.

"Your name has been submitted for consideration to join the President's Committee for People with Intellectual Disabilities here in Washington. Is that something you'd be interested in?" he asked.

"Uh, yeah," I replied, though I had never heard of the PCPID.

"There will be an extensive background check and vetting process," Jones continued. "People rarely get to this level without making somebody mad. Is there any reason someone might say you shouldn't be on this committee?"

I always knew my permanent record from elementary school would come back to bite me.

When I became board president of The Arc of Texas, a reporter interviewed me, and I suggested that a good quality of life was as important for people living in institutions as it was for those living in the community. Advocates who wanted to close all institutions said that was heresy. Few people knew I volunteered in the Sunday chapel services at the Denton State Supported Living Center, the state's largest institution.

"You may find an article where I speak kindly about people in institutions," I confessed my sin.

"That's fine," he replied. "We want people with a wide variety of opinions."

"That's good to know," I said with relief as another issue came to mind. "I'm also an evangelical Christian from Texas who often votes Republican. Is that a problem?"

"Don't worry about it. We've got a few of those too!" Jones laughed out loud. I didn't know if he meant they had Christians, Republicans, or both. Regardless, I was probably a little different from most of their other appointees.

The vetting process was unimaginable. In addition to full background and criminal checks, I disclosed every piece of financial minutia that existed. My CPA never asked for that level of detail. I felt totally naked and exposed, so I hoped they enjoyed the view.

The holidays turned into 2011 with no word from Washington. I emailed Jones several times to check on the status and always received his standard reply.

"The process is still underway, and remember, don't say a word to anyone about your nomination. We don't want anything out to the public until the final decisions are made."

"Congratulations, Clay, you're now an official member of the PCPID," Jones said when my phone rang on May 3, 2011. "We were going to announce the appointees a couple of weeks ago but were told to put everything on hold due to what happened yesterday."

Osama bin Laden had been killed the day before, and our announcement was a nonstarter compared to eliminating the world's most notorious terrorist.

The PCPID had one mandated responsibility: to issue an annual report to the president. It could be on whatever topic the committee chose, but a report must be issued.

Our report for 2011 focused on avoiding budget cuts to programs that people needed for survival, such as employment, education, health care, and long-term services. Each section included the committee's point of view on the need, followed by a real-life testimony from someone who benefited from that support.

The testimonies came from regular citizens outside the committee, except one—mine. I was told that no active member of PCPID had ever shared their story in the Report to the President. My passage focused on long-term services and supports:

My wife and I have three daughters, including identical twins who both have severe intellectual disabilities and autism. When my twins were eight years old, the stress of raising two children who had constant meltdowns, bit and scratched everyone around them, and were not toilet trained had reached the boiling point. My wife and I fought daily, and our oldest daughter was witnessing the loss of her family and childhood.

As my twins continued to sit for years on waiting lists for community-based Medicaid waiver services, and with no other options at hand, I contacted a local advocacy group in search of a place who could take our twins. As we clearly were in crisis mode, we qualified for state funds available through our school system to provide respite support. We were approved for that support, and our first attendant joined us three weeks later. When she arrived, the stress on my family was reduced in an unimaginable way, and our children could continue being raised by those who love them most.

These funds provided support until our twins reached the top of one of the Medicaid waiver waiting lists, which now enables their respite care. If that support is removed, I have no doubt my family will fracture, and we will be forced to consider state placement options, which will not only increase the cost of my children's care, but literally break up our family. Like all parents, we look forward to the day that all our children are living under their own roofs. Until then, our children deserve as traditional a childhood as possible, and the cornerstone of that childhood is grounded in our family staying together. Medicaid waivers are critical in making that happen.

While most families guarded their privacy like gold, my family's dirty laundry was published and bound in a report to the President of the United States and archived in American history. Discretion was not my strong suit.

THE EXECUTIVE DIRECTOR OF a national advocacy organization walked the PCPID through a presentation that concluded that people with IDD wanted to live at home with their parents as long as possible. This was based on statistics that showed most people with disabilities lived with their relatives. It created the illusion that parents wanted their financial obligations and physical stress to last forever.

"That's the most ridiculous thing I ever heard," I said into the table microphone in front of fifty people. The room went dead silent, shocked that a committee member would challenge a supposed expert in the disability field.

"The reason so many adults with IDD live at home with their parents," I explained, "is not because it's everyone's favorite choice. It's because they have no other options."

"Clay is right," said Bob, an ex-officio member of the committee from the Department of Transportation. Ex-officios said little during the meetings, but Bob had a son with Down syndrome and immediately backed up my response. This changed the tone of the room as others chimed in with their concerns as well.

"THE REASON SO MANY ADULTS WITH IDD LIVE AT HOME WITH THEIR PARENTS," I EXPLAINED, "IS NOT BECAUSE IT'S EVERYONE'S FAVORITE CHOICE. IT'S BECAUSE THEY HAVE NO OTHER OPTIONS."

"We have a thirty-minute meeting scheduled with the new commissioner of DADS," said Amy, the government affairs director of The Arc of Texas. "Can you join us?"

DADS was Texas's Department of Aging and Disability Services. Invitations to meetings like this were a nice benefit of being board president of The Arc.

"I'm a bureaucrat; meanwhile, you and your families deal with these challenges nonstop," Chris said after he sat down at the head of the table. We didn't hear humble statements like that very often. Our thirty-minute meeting lasted an hour and a half as he heard stories from each person at the table.

A few months later, the commissioner attended a meeting at the Denton institution and wanted to speak with Dallas-area advocates before he returned to Austin. The group included Kate, a young woman with Down syndrome. Kate described how her job leasing out beverage machines added value to other people's lives. She also shared about her love for her family and God.

"God knew what He was doing when He gave each of us unique skills and abilities," I said when Kate was done. "Our job is to help each other identify and maximize those abilities."

The commissioner was silent. His mind was elsewhere, and I wondered if talking about God had made him uncomfortable.

Chris walked up during a break and described a family member with a disability. "God allowed me to have this job for a reason, yet I'm not sure how to help my family," he shared.

"God puts us in specific places at specific times," I replied. "The frustration is that we don't know why, and we never know God's timing. My suggestion is to see where He leads."

Chris was promoted to the number two position over all Health Services a few years later.

"I may apply for one of the new state advisory committees," I mentioned to Chris one day. My term on the President's Committee had ended, and I needed a new place to cause trouble. "Which one do you think I should go for?"

"I'm going to name you chairman of whichever one you pick, so you tell me," he replied. I chaired the IDD System Redesign Advisory Committee (SRAC), created by the Texas legislature, for six and a half years.

"Hey Clay, are you available for dinner on Tuesday night?" asked Jon, the new commissioner of DADS. He was in Dallas for a conference, and we got together at a local steakhouse.

"I appreciate working with you and the agency," I said when our steaks came out. "The unique access is not lost on me."

"Clay, we like you because you're fair," he replied as he cut into his filet. "You fight for what you think is right but also respect people who have different experiences and points of view. You also appreciate the challenges we face at the agency. Sometimes I think you know how we operate better than we do!"

"Thanks, Jon, that's very kind," I replied. "I have a dirty little secret," I continued. "People think all my advocacy work is for the greater good. That's a nice side benefit, but Paige and Mia are the reasons for what I do. Not every issue I push will benefit them, but they're the only reason I'm here."

"Of course they are," he said. "You're smart and learned how to work through the system for their benefit. If I were a special needs kid, I'd want you to be my dad."

I paused for a moment, humbled by the nicest compliment I'd ever received.

TOP 5 "TO-DOS" FOR FAMILIES WITH DISABILITIES

"CLAY, A FRIEND OF MINE, HAS A SON WITH AUTISM, and it's been tough on her and her family. He's getting older, and they're at the end of their rope. Would you mind talking to them?"

"I'd be happy to," was my answer to this question a hundred times over. "Here's my contact card. Have them reach out to me." Maybe one person in ten ever contacted me. Many people would rather admire a problem and complain about life than ask for help.

To help families who were reluctant to reach out, I developed the Disability Top 5, the five most important things to do when raising children with disabilities.

#1. GET HELP AT HOME.

THIS WAS FAR AND AWAY THE MOST IMPORTANT OF THE FIVE. When we moved away from Memphis, Carole and I left all our support systems behind. Twenty years later, we had three daughters, two with disabilities, only one of us at home during the day, and zero help.

Our first attempt to hire a nanny was a flaming disaster. We replied to an ad that a young woman posted looking for a mother's helper position. The blonde sixteen-year-old drove her new BMW to meet our family and brought her mother with her. We thought the interview went well until Carole called the next day and offered her the job.

"You should have warned my daughter before we came over," the girl's mother told Carole when she answered the phone. "You will not find anyone to help you. Nobody can handle children like yours."

Devastated, we stopped looking for years.

"I can't do it anymore," Carole said one night several years later.

"Okay," I replied. "When I get back from Austin, we'll try to find help." An Arc of Texas board meeting was the next day.

"Carole's about to go crazy, and I have no idea what to do," I said to Rona, The Arc's head of education advocacy. "The stress is unbearable, and I don't see an end to it."

"Has your school told you about the noneducation funds?" she asked. "They can be used for hiring in-home help."

"Never heard of them," I replied. We still had a lot to learn.

That night, I got on the internet and discovered that there were state funds available through our school system that could be used for respite support. This was news as well to Kellie and Christina, the twins' elementary school principal and teacher, but they were happy to fill out the paperwork. Our application was approved by a social services committee a week later.

Nathalie walked in our door less than a month after we learned about the state funds. Fresh air. Peace. Sleep. Smiles. Laughter. These returned to our home.

"She looks like Gabriella from *High School Musical*," eleven-year-old Blaire shouted on the day Nathalie arrived. A student at Texas Women's University, the state funds made her an employee of our school system, a nice résumé builder for when she received her teaching degree.

Nathalie worked three hours every afternoon when Paige and Mia got home from school. She changed pull-ups, prepared snacks, and played games with the twins while Carole cooked dinner and helped Blaire with her homework. When I got home from work, I would take over for Nathalie and maintain the momentum.

"You're responsible for making sure your home is clean," my mother told my older sister when we were young. "However, that doesn't mean you have to clean it."

That truth applies to many aspects of our lives. If we were comfortable paying someone to cut our grass or mop our floors, what was wrong with asking someone to help maintain peace in our home? These people had stronger skills than ours, and shame on us for not hiring them and helping them feed their families.

Martyrdom, carrying the burden alone, was not sexy and would have destroyed our family.

MARTYRDOM, CARRYING THE BURDEN ALONE, WAS NOT SEXY AND WOULD HAVE DESTROYED OUR FAMILY.

#2. Get help through the state's Medicaid waiver program.

Every state has Medicaid programs for people and families with disabilities that waives the regular eligibility requirements and provides in-home support, therapies, and respite. In many cases, they also fund residential supports that enable the recipient to live on their own. These programs are not entitlements, which means that state legislators decide how much to spend and how many people can participate. Since demand is often greater than supply, many states have a waiting list that could be decades long.

When we found out about the Texas waiver programs, we signed up the twins for two of them, the Medically Dependent Children's Program (MDCP) and Home & Community-Based Services (HCS).

"Paige and Mia are getting MDCP!" Carole exclaimed when I got home one evening. The twins were older, and the nighttime routine had become difficult, so we hired someone to work from 6 p.m. to 9 p.m. to round out the night. For the first time in ten years, Carole and I could go on dates again! Blaire was a leader on her high school dance squad, and God's perfect timing enabled Carole and me to attend all her halftime football performances. It also allowed me to be the team's stadium announcer for three straight years. More than respite, getting help at home led to some of our most cherished memories.

Over time, more than thirty ladies came to our home and helped us build a life that was almost normal. Carole and I joked that more women had seen me in my pajamas than Hugh Hefner.

This robust sample of in-home help led to an unexpected observation: the better attendants had tattoos. Though there were exceptions, body art was a pretty good indicator of success and longevity. We theorized that tattoos often indicated life experiences outside the mainstream, which made them empathetic toward others on the fringe. Lord knew our family was on the fringe.

"CLAY, WE GOT A CALL FROM AUSTIN," Carole called me on a Friday morning at work. "They said that Paige and Mia no longer qualify for MDCP, and it ends next month. You need to handle this." Carole's mom had been in and out of the hospital for months, and Carole didn't need this on her plate too.

"I'm on it," I replied. Lots of kids with MDCP had been dropped as the state redefined medical dependency. In the twins' case, their dependence on seizure and behavior meds was not enough.

For years, we'd pieced together a manageable life based on in-home support. The twins were years away before reaching the top of the HCS waiting list, so this was a cataclysmic disaster. A decade of advocacy was about to be tested.

At 10:20 a.m., I placed two phone calls, one to an administrator at our county's disability support agency and the other to Health Services in Austin. In a calm, cheerful voice, with no stress at all, both people heard the same thing.

"Hey, we found out that Paige and Mia no longer qualify for MDCP. I totally understand and, to be honest, was kind of expecting it. That said, here's what you need to know. On the morning after their last day of service, if there isn't a replacement program in place, I'm going to pack their bags, drive them to the Denton State Supported Living Center, walk them into the lobby, tell whoever is there that they have two new residents, and then walk out. That's exactly what is going to happen. Let me know what you want to do!"

Both gentlemen said, "Let me make some calls," and hung up the phone. No requests or demands were made; they simply learned my plan. The ball was now in their court.

Advocacy taught me three things that were relevant to this situation. First, the state didn't want to institutionalize two fourteen-year-old girls who had a loving family willing to care for them. The paperwork would be immense.

Second, there were things called "HCS diversion slots." Separate from the regular HCS waiting list, these diverted someone at imminent risk of institutionalization into a community-based setting through an HCS slot. All doubt was removed that Paige and Mia were at imminent risk.

Third, the state did its best work when it had a crisis to solve. With decades-long waiting lists and a stifling bureaucracy, the state was not designed to help a family plan. However, when someone was in dire need, people in public service would do everything possible to help them. Losing support for Paige and Mia would not be our crisis; it would be the state's crisis.

THIRD, THE STATE DID ITS BEST WORK WHEN
IT HAD A CRISIS TO SOLVE. . . WHEN SOMEONE WAS
IN DIRE NEED, PEOPLE IN PUBLIC SERVICE WOULD
DO EVERYTHING POSSIBLE TO HELP THEM.

Around 3:30 that afternoon, I received a call from Austin that Paige and Mia qualified for two diversion slots that would be available in time to avoid a break in service. The state solved its crisis.

#3. TAKE ADVANTAGE OF ALL COMMUNITY-SPONSORED PROGRAMS.

FAMILIES WITH DISABILITIES survived on word-of-mouth about programs that would reduce stress and help our children develop. HEROES, Friday Night Respite, and the dance studio when they were younger were prime examples.

Discovering The Arc introduced us to April and the outstanding children's programs she had for kids like ours. Meanwhile, volunteering enabled us to meet other advocates and disability-focused nonprofits. Camp Summit was an overnight program that served clients with a wide array of disabilities for an entire week. For several years, Mia and Paige would go to Camp Summit for spring break while Carole, Blaire, and I headed off to a resort for a few days, stress-free.

Many times, we were told that people who worked with our twins benefited from the experience. God gave us two special gifts with Paige and Mia, and we had a moral obligation to share our gifts with as many people as possible!

#4. FIND A CHURCH HOME THAT WELCOMES YOUR UNIQUE FAMILY.

CAROLE AND I WERE HEAVILY ENGAGED in church from the day we got married. It helped us understand God, our relationship with Him, and His plan for our lives. It also strengthened our marriage during tough times and helped us appreciate Christ's sacrifice for us. These were important, and we wanted all our children exposed to the church.

"Paige and Mia's Sunday School teacher called today," Carole said one afternoon. "They want one of us to be in their class at all times to help manage them."

We'd been members of the church before the twins were born and participated in adult fellowship and a variety of ministries. For several summers, I was the only man to work at Vacation Bible School, a move that impressed quite a few stay-at-home moms. That phone call, however, sent us to another church the next Sunday.

Carole's only break during the week was on Sunday mornings, and she cherished it. It gave her a chance to catch her breath, relax, and fellowship with other adult couples. Telling her to give that up broke her heart.

Our children were tough, and we were happy to reciprocate at any church that would take them. However, expecting us to serve in the children's ministry with our own children every week because of their disabilities was inappropriate. Carole's passion was women's ministry, and mine was missions. Neither one of us was gifted in elementary education, which is why we appreciated those who were.

Two things were required for a church to serve children with disabilities: a desire from the pastor and leadership to do so and the resources to make it happen. Many churches took the approach we saw in secular society. Paige and Mia were welcome to participate if they were potty-trained, didn't have challenging behaviors, and followed directions like everyone else. In other words, our children could come to God's house if no one had to deal with their disability.

TWO THINGS WERE REQUIRED FOR A CHURCH
TO SERVE CHILDREN WITH DISABILITIES:
A DESIRE FROM THE PASTOR AND LEADERSHIP
TO DO SO AND THE RESOURCES
TO MAKE IT HAPPEN.

Stonebriar Community Church, led by Pastor Chuck Swindoll, was our next church home. Swindoll's grandson was on the autism spectrum, and Stonebriar had an excellent special needs ministry. Through the church, we learned about an organization called Joni & Friends, a ministry that hosted family camps around the country.

"This week gives us hope for the rest of the year," I mentioned to a camp leader. Her daughter took Paige and Mia for fun activities each day, Blaire enjoyed events with kids her age, and Carole and I fellowshipped with other parents. We went to "family camp" outside Houston for six years in a row, and it became a highlight of our summers.

"PRESTONWOOD'S FAMILY APPRECIATION DINNER is next week for families with kids who have disabilities," Carole's friend mentioned to her one day. Intrigued, Carole called the church and signed us up.

Prestonwood Baptist was a 40,000-member megachurch with huge influence in both community service and politics. With multiple sites in the area, another church pastor once referred to Prestonwood as "the church that ate Dallas." They'd started a special needs ministry a few years earlier and hosted an annual outreach dinner.

"This is one of our favorite events of the year," Pastor Jack Graham told the audience seated around cloth-covered tables in the church's massive lobby.

With an impressive special-needs ministry and a Saturday evening service that enabled us to sleep in on Sunday mornings, we decided to join. I became a deacon a few years later. When a new children's wing was built, a hand-painted portrait of Mia working with one of her teachers adorned the lobby.

My disability advocacy wasn't limited to elected officials and bureaucrats, and sometimes the ordained got a piece of me too.

"Which disabilities should we serve—all of them?" a pastor asked me one day.

"As a matter of fact, yes," I laughed in response. That was like asking what races he should serve. Perhaps he could start with the people God created. Oh, that would be everybody!

The "Roman Road" was a collection of verses from the Book of Romans that described the path to salvation through Jesus Christ. In that same spirit, I penned "The Disability Road," using specific Bible verses that share God's perspective on people with disabilities:

- God designed everyone individually (Psalm 139:13-16)
- Including those of us with disabilities (Exodus 4:10-11)
- Thus, disabilities were not punishment but to display God's power (John 9:1-3)
- And should be treated with honor (1 Corinthians 12:21-26)
- The way we honor people is to serve them (1 Peter 4:10)

- Particularly those who cannot repay us (Luke 14:12-14)
- And defend their cause, maintain their rights, and rescue them from harm (Psalm 82:3-4)

#5. GET INVOLVED.

"MY FRIENDS ASK ME ALL THE TIME what you do for a living," twenty-year-old Blaire laughed one day. "I tell them I have absolutely no idea!"

Though I knew thousands of people, 95 percent had no idea what I did for a living, yet everyone knew what I did for free: disability advocacy.

"I think it's great your employer lets you spend so much time doing advocacy work," Rick, our lawyer, said one afternoon.

"Thanks," I smiled in response, "but I never asked them. I'm not sure what 'no' would sound like anyway!"

MANY PARENTS, ESPECIALLY FATHERS,
SAID THEY DIDN'T HAVE TIME TO GET
INVOLVED BECAUSE OF THEIR CAREERS,
WHICH MADE NO SENSE TO ME.

Many parents, especially fathers, said they didn't have time to get involved because of their careers, which made no sense to me. We were a single income family raising not one—but two—children with severe disabilities, and figured it out. That said, I had deep empathy for families, particularly single parents, who got paid by the hour and did not have my flexibility. There was never a conflict between my paying job and volunteer efforts. I made sure both responsibilities were met and never used one as an excuse for the other.

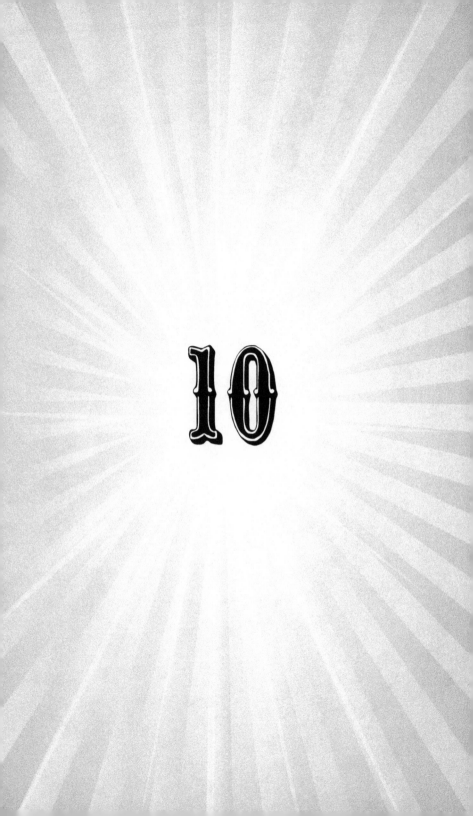

THE CIRCUS ON THE ROAD

I have died and gone to hell, I thought as we pulled into West Memphis, Arkansas.

The I-40 and I-55 merge in West Memphis was under construction for forty years. We drove from Dallas to Cincinnati one Thanksgiving and found ourselves in that colossal mess. It was 10:30 p.m., and we had another hour before getting to our hotel. The cold, pounding rain made it almost impossible to see the road from our minivan. Four-year-old Paige and Mia made it deadlier by screaming at the top of their lungs from their car seats. Carole was upset and frustrated while Blaire tried to disappear in the back.

Determined never to let a night like that happen again, six months later, we rented an RV for a trip to Disney World. We rented a house near the park, but the two-day drive each way was surprisingly fun. I drove with everyone else unleashed in the back, able to walk around, play, watch movies on TV, and, most important, use the onboard bathroom.

"That went well," Carole and I agreed when we returned. Travel was something normal families did, so we looked for an RV and found a used twenty-four-footer that was perfect.

"Hard right!" became my common warning from the driver's seat of our minivan-on-steroids as Carole and Blaire laughed in the back and grabbed the twins for dear life with every turn.

SOMETHING'S NOT RIGHT, I thought as we drove down I-45 to Houston on a Saturday afternoon for our annual Joni & Friends vacation. The engine sputtered for about a minute, the dials flipped to the right, then left, and the engine died at seventy miles per hour. I coasted the dead ship onto the shoulder of the road, enough for the right tires to reach the grass.

It was a hot and humid 102 degrees on that July 2, and we were dead in the water, out in the middle of nowhere.

"My cell phone has bars," I said with relief. "That's a good sign." I called the number on the back of our Good Sam's card, the AAA for RVs.

"I have no idea where we are," I told the operator. He asked me to find the closest mile marker, so I left the family and walked several hundred feet ahead. The temperature was rising fast in our now un-air-conditioned tin can.

"Listen, my wife and three young daughters are with me," I explained. "Two of my kids have severe autism and don't realize what's happened. We can't let them out of the RV because they'll run onto the interstate, so it's going to get bad out here if we can't get their movies playing soon!"

"I understand, sir. We'll get a technician there as soon as we can," he replied with empathy in his voice.

Carole and I noticed something while we waited. Paige and Mia were unbelievably calm. They didn't cry or have a meltdown and were not the least bit upset to be stranded with no entertainment. We couldn't decide if they sensed the tension and decided to be calm or if the rising heat in the van zapped their energy. Either way, we'd take it.

The tow truck pulled up thirty minutes later. The mechanic checked the engine and diagnosed a blown alternator.

"First things first," he said as he hitched us up. "We need to get you off the interstate." He had room for us in the back seat of his truck as he towed us to the next exit and parked our RV under the awning of an abandoned service station.

"I'm hoping our auto parts store three exits down has an alternator," he said. "Otherwise, you're here until Monday."

We envisioned dying of old age as we awaited his return. We called the camp, which offered to send someone to pick up the family, but it was still early, so we decided to wait. We'd call back if this became an overnighter.

"That was fast!" I told the mechanic when he returned forty-five minutes later.

"You were lucky," he replied. "This was the last alternator they had for this model, and we got it," he said as he installed it.

That day could have been a nightmare on several levels. It might have taken someone hours to help us as we sweltered in the boiling heat. The girls could have been out of control, or the auto shop could have been out of alternators, and we could have been stranded for days. Instead, God had us back on the road in less than two hours.

"Marta, can I ask you a favor that I cannot ask another person on the planet?" I said to my sister. We were on the balcony of her condo overlooking the Ohio River in Cincinnati. Our mother's funeral had been earlier that day, and people were gathered at my sister's place for a reception.

"Umm, okay," she replied, appropriately cautious. Since the day I was born, she knew to expect the unexpected.

"Can you and Mike come to Dallas and watch our kids, so I can take my wife on a vacation?" I asked, knowing this was a huge request.

Typical families could ask relatives to watch their kids for a parents' getaway, but it was unheard of in the special needs community, particularly when the children had severe disabilities. It was like asking a twenty-year-old girl to guard a men's maximum-security prison alone in her bikini.

TYPICAL FAMILIES COULD ASK RELATIVES TO
WATCH THEIR KIDS FOR A PARENTS' GETAWAY,
BUT IT WAS UNHEARD OF IN THE SPECIAL
NEEDS COMMUNITY.

"Let me talk to Mike," she replied, "but we may be able to do that." The next day she said they would be happy to watch the kids, and we started to plan a trip for a year later.

A lot of engineering was needed to pull this off. The first was timing. We had to work around Marta and Mike's schedule, and it needed to be during the school year so they didn't have to be on duty 24/7. Decent weather would maximize the use of our swimming pool. We settled on September, which happened to be our wedding anniversary.

Marta and Mike flew in on Wednesday to learn the ropes a few days before our Saturday departure to Rome, Italy. We walked them through the awakening process, introduced them to the school bus driver, showed them where to drop Blaire at school, and they met the host of after-school activities. They were both Procter & Gamble executives with adult children of their own, so Carole and I weren't worried at all.

The room in our boutique hotel was two blocks away from the Colosseum and large by European standards. We basked in the majesty of the Vatican and Sistine Chapel, stepped back into ancient times at the Roman Forum and Pantheon, reveled in the beauty of Villa Borghese, and took a day trip to Tuscany. Our week in Rome was the vacation of a lifetime.

When we returned home and walked into the house, Mike whispered in Marta's ear, yielding a surprised look on her face. "How was everything?" I asked.

"It was great," my sister replied, "but we have some bad news."

"You wrecked the Mustang?!" I reacted in hyper panic. I walked to the garage to see the damage on my custom-built 2005 black Mustang GT convertible.

"No, we didn't wreck your car," Marta replied, resisting the temptation to smack my head. "Cheese died. Like, now."

Cheese, Blaire's pet guinea pig since he was a piglet, was getting on in age. Our return home must have been overwhelming and was his cue to check out. In typical Boatright fashion, our once-in-a-lifetime vacation ended with an untimely death.

"We'd like to run an idea by you," Marta said a while later. "Mike and I had a great time with the girls this week. It was really nice to spend time with and get to know them. Living far away, we haven't been able to help you guys very much, so if you're interested, we'd like to do this again. We can't do it every year, but maybe every other year."

The magnitude of that offer was off the charts.

"Oh my God, thank you!" Carole exclaimed. It never crossed our minds to ask if they'd watch our kids like this again, much less three more times over the next six years.

That was 2007. Canals highlighted our trip to Venice two years later, and an overnight train to Vienna, Austria, allowed Carole to see the Lipizzaner horses she'd always admired. In 2011, our plane landed in Istanbul, Turkey, where Europe and Asia meet at the Bosphorus Strait—a key locale in James Bond's *From Russia with Love*. A day trip to Izmir, once known as Ephesus, enabled us to stand on the same stage where the

Apostle Paul preached. Istanbul also put Carole's negotiation skills to work at the Grand Bizarre, where she argued with a merchant for forty-five minutes over the price of a scarf. When they were done, he would have given it to her for free to make her go away.

"Okay, this may sound crazy," I told Carole, as we planned our 2013 trip. "What do you think about Russia?"

"Well, that's different," she replied. "We have unconventional kids, so why not unconventional vacations?"

We waited nervously in line at passport control in Moscow. For weeks I envisioned armed guards demanding, "Your papers!" with security hauling us away if anything was odd. When we reached the booth, the uniformed agent glanced at us quickly, stamped our passports, and handed them back in less than fifteen seconds. My fantasies were dashed once again.

We walked through the churches and armory of the Kremlin, mesmerized by sites we'd only seen in action movies. Red Square and GUM department store, however, did not compare to the beauty of the underground subway stations, where colorful mosaic tiles and statues created mini museums at every stop.

A train took us to Saint Petersburg, formerly known as Leningrad. The cultural capital of Russia, it was the seat of power for the czars and was home to some of the most beautiful palaces we'd seen. A solemnness cloaked the room of the Winter Palace, where the Bolsheviks violently took control of the government in 1917 and ushered in the Soviet era.

"YOU MAY BE THE ONLY ELEVEN-YEAR-OLD IN HISTORY to attend her first presidential inauguration and mob riot on the exact same day!" I told Blaire over dinner in Chinatown in DC during our trip to President Obama's inauguration.

Our instructions for the ceremony were to arrive at the Purple Gate entrance at 6:00 a.m., four hours in advance of the event. We left the dorm room we'd rented at Georgetown

University in darkness and arrived to find thousands of people already there with the gates closed.

By seven, the crowd behind us went as far as the eye could see. Around eight, stories of people jam-packed in an underground highway tunnel over a mile away started to circulate. An hour later, the chanting started. "One, two, three, four, we don't want to wait no more. Five, six, seven, eight, open up the Purple Gate."

We heard the ceremony start on the loudspeakers, and the crowd became agitated. Thousands of people were sandwiched together, body on body, and I told Blaire not to let go of my hand under any circumstances. Around 10:15—more than four hours after we'd arrived—a trickle of people ran on the other side of the fence. While most of the crowd was focused on being mad, Blaire and I inched our way toward the gate, where two of the eight security lines were open.

We made it through security at 10:30 as Vice-President Biden was sworn in. Blaire and I broke into a full-speed sprint toward the Capitol, and in three minutes, we hit a wall of bodies on the grounds. We maneuvered our way through the crowd and crawled under a bush with other invitees, peeking through the branches toward the building. This was not the way we'd planned it, but we were on the property at 10:35 when Obama was sworn in as president.

An official investigation was launched to understand what the media labeled the "Purple Tunnel of Doom." Tens of thousands of ticket holders never made it through the gate, including elected leaders and congressional staffers. Blaire and I felt lucky under the circumstances.

"It was crazy," I told Carole back home. "But it was great spending one-on-one time with Blaire. Since Martin Luther King Day is a long weekend and not a major family holiday, what would you think about me taking Blaire on a trip every year at this time?"

It was a big ask of the mother who would be left behind, and I would never have mentioned it if we didn't have help with the twins.

"I think she would enjoy it," Carole said to my surprise. It helped that our Rome trip had been eighteen months earlier, with Venice and Vienna planned for later that year.

"Blaire, here's an idea," I told her later that night. "Every year over the Martin Luther King holiday, we'll go anywhere in the country you want to go. What do you think?"

Without taking a breath, she shouted, "Hollywood!"

Our daddy-daughter trips became legendary. Hollywood and Los Angeles in 2010, followed by New York City the next year. The plane taxied out for our trip to the Big Apple when I turned to Blaire and said, "You do know these trips aren't really for you, right?"

Blaire smiled and said, "I know, Daddy."

Each trip featured a formal dinner and a live show of some kind. We ate dinner overlooking Times Square from the top of the Marriott Marquis in Manhattan and later saw the musical *Memphis* on Broadway.

In 2012, my fourteen-year-old daughter wanted to go to Las Vegas, which included front-row seats to Penn & Teller, along with personal introductions afterward.

"Daddy, I think Vegas is a lot more fun when you're an adult. I want to come back when I turn twenty-one." Blaire was a very insightful teenager.

We passed on an invitation to the 2013 Presidential Inauguration for fear of repeating the Purple Gate fiasco. Instead, we expanded our borders a bit and went to London.

Our MLK-weekend trips were always in late January, so we were accustomed to cold weather. London, buried under its biggest snowstorm in twenty years on the day after we arrived, however, was unique. Undeterred, we hit the must-see sights such as both Houses of Parliament and Platform 9 3/4 at the

Kings Cross train station, where Harry Potter caught the Hogwarts Express.

Buckingham Palace had recently opened for tours for the first time in history. They were at sporadic times and were announced only a day or so in advance. I checked the internet, saw it was open that weekend, and grabbed a spot.

Security guards led fifteen of us into the palace, where photographs were not allowed. For an hour and a half, we toured the Throne Room, Picture Gallery, Grand Ballroom, and the Queen's Study, including secret passages that Her Majesty used to move from one room to another without being seen. The tour ended with champagne in the palace's Entry Hall.

"I've traveled around the world, but this is pretty darn cool," I said to Blaire as we enjoyed our beverages. "You'll attend work meetings in the future where everyone will be asked to name something they've done that no one else in the room has done. Drinking champagne in Buckingham Palace will be yours!"

11

TRANSITIONS

CAROLE AND I WERE HIDING in our home office one night. Paige and Mia were watching TV upstairs with their attendants, and Blaire was at Oklahoma State University, but we were not relaxed.

"This is what it's going to be like for the rest of our lives," Carole said. Living with our youngest children forever had not been our plan.

"I'll start looking for a group home," I replied. A decade of volunteering in the Dallas-area disability community meant we knew everybody, and everybody knew us. Surely, our strong relationships with service providers would come in handy. I couldn't have been more wrong.

"I wish we could help, but we don't have any openings," was the most common response. Texas's poor reimbursement rates for services meant demand exceeded supply, and providers had no incentive to add new clients.

"Paige and Mia don't fit our model" was the polite way to say that our children were too disabled for some providers. It was cheaper to serve people with stronger skill sets because the challenges required fewer staff members. The dirty little secret of the disability support system was that those with more significant needs were less likely to get the help they required.

"For a year and a half, every service provider has turned us down," I told Fern, an executive with a local disability agency.

THE DIRTY LITTLE SECRET OF THE DISABILITY
SUPPORT SYSTEM WAS THAT THOSE WITH
MORE SIGNIFICANT NEEDS WERE LESS LIKELY
TO GET THE HELP THEY REQUIRED.

"Have you talked to Avid?" she asked, referring to a provider I didn't know.

"Never heard of 'em," I replied as I wrote down their name.

"Have you talked to Avid?" another provider asked me a few hours later.

"That name has come up twice in the same day!" I laughed. "Sounds like we need to talk!"

Shelly and Cody, the husband-and-wife team who owned Avid, came to our house a week later to meet the girls. Carole and I were nervous. Paige's unexplained weight loss and emotional breakdowns added to the angst. The owners, however, impressed us with their honesty about the challenges and blessings of serving people with disabilities.

"We have another young lady who needs a home as well," they said after a couple of hours. "We're willing to take a chance to see if it can work."

"I'm nervous about this," Carole said a week before they moved. "They're not even seventeen yet!"

"It will be fine," I replied, though I was nervous as well. We were physically and emotionally out of gas. There was no alternative. It was the week before New Year's, Paige had been in the hospital, and we barely survived another Christmas disaster. January 3 was moving day, and it couldn't come soon enough.

David was another special-needs father who'd formed a nonprofit to create more group homes in Plano. So, we connected David with Avid to create the twin's first home away from home, less than two miles away.

Avid employed two caregivers to care for three nonverbal clients with unique behaviors during waking hours, with one sleeping overnight. Once the routine was established, Karmen became their house manager and full-time caregiver.

"Just because they have a disability doesn't mean they need to dress like it," Karmen told us. She was a few years older than Blaire and had a strong sense of style. Unlike group homes that required staff to wear scrubs, Karmen's eye for fashion showed through for herself and the girls. We would go out and people would notice the twins' fashionable dresses and bling. The girls knew they looked good, and it affirmed that their care was strong.

Many parents of children with severe disabilities thought their parental rights automatically continued when their child became an adult. Those rights do not continue, nor should they. Everyone, no matter their IQ, becomes an independent legal adult when they turn eighteen. Protecting an individual's decision-making rights is a top priority, and while it may be inconvenient for parents, a complicated process for taking them away is necessary.

Many disability advocates preferred *supported decision-making*, where trusted advisors provided guidance for the individual to make their own choices. That would not work for

Paige and Mia because their skill set required someone else to make the important decisions.

The process of becoming their guardians started six months before their eighteenth birthday. We collected doctor recommendations and school records while the court appointed an ad litem lawyer to represent the twins. Their ad litem told us she often spent hours with her clients to prepare her report for the judge. She was with Paige and Mia for ten minutes.

The ward attends the court hearing for the judge to meet the individual and make his or her own assessment. For our case, the twins' ad litem lawyer asked the court not to require Paige and Mia's attendance. Because they could not participate, it would disrupt their school schedule and could cause unnecessary stress. The judge agreed.

Carole and I showed up at the courthouse in suits and were ready to spend as much time as necessary explaining why Mia and Paige needed guardians and why we would be the best ones. The judge sat on his bench fifteen feet away and didn't ask a single question. Rick, our lawyer, did all the talking, and it was over in less than three minutes.

Does the ward reside/live with the guardian? This question was on the guardianship report we sent to the court every year.

If No, please state the number of times you visited the ward in the past year.

I thought for a second and wrote fifty-five, though it may have been more.

That simple question hit me deep. We were told it was rare for a parent or guardian to visit every week, year after year. I understood that every family situation was unique, but that surprised me. Our weekly visits ensured the house was in order and everyone was healthy. Paige and Mia enjoyed our time together, and truth be known, our visits every weekend were less for the twins and more for me.

I'd attended over a thousand Sunday morning church services in my life, yet never once left refreshed. Most often, I left reminded that I was a sinner and generally sucked. My rejuvenation came from our visits with Paige and Mia every week, and I wouldn't have traded them for the world.

A typical visit involved doing nothing—absolutely nothing. For hours, we might sit on a love seat. Mia would pull a hair tie off her head and put it in my hand to retie her ponytail, so she could immediately pull it out again. That sequence would play out sixty times. More important, for three hours or so every week, our daughters wanted to sit by and be engaged with us.

The group home brought unexpected relief from the most dreaded season for the Boatright Circus: the holidays. As Hell Month approached that first year the girls were in the home, Carole and I tested a new strategy.

On Thanksgiving Day, we brought the twins home with Blaire and had their favorite foods as a low-key event focused on them. Afterward, we took them back to their house and enjoyed our traditional Thanksgiving a few days later. It was our most relaxing holiday in twenty years.

This new approach to the holidays was great for everyone. Most important, Carole enjoyed a peace that had eluded her for decades, while Blaire got a small glimpse of how normal families lived.

"I WANT TO GO BACK TO WORK FULL TIME," Carole told me after the holidays. She was working part time at Sur La Table, a high-end cookware store, where I was confident she spent more using her employee discount than she earned in pay.

"That's a great idea!" I replied. Returning to work would be a huge step for her to regain a sense of normalcy.

Carole's updated résumé and LinkedIn profile described how years of volunteer and part-time experience would be valuable to potential employers. She responded to ads and reached out to several contacts, including Katy, a fellow dance mom she'd known for a long time. Katy needed someone to fill an inside sales and customer service position at the company where she worked, a technology provider in the hospitality industry. Carole jumped at the opportunity.

"I don't feel very good," Carole told me one morning while getting ready for work. She'd been on the job about six months, and things were finally starting to click. Not one to ignore a strange pain in her stomach, she called her doctor and made an appointment.

12

COWBOYS AND DOCTORS

Dr. Kathryn, the OB/GYN who'd performed the twins' hysterectomies, walked into the waiting room after Carole's surgery. She had a serious look on her face. The stomach pain resulted in another Boatright hysterectomy, but during surgery, Dr. Kathryn discovered something she hadn't anticipated: ovarian cancer. She connected us with Dr. Allen, a gynecological oncologist, and Carole went under the knife again.

"It looks like we got it all," Allen told us after the next surgery. "We'll check you regularly, but it's looking good."

Six months later, in January 2018, Carole's scan showed no cancer. What a relief! All our kids were out of the house, Carole enjoyed her job, a life of normal that we'd never experienced was on the horizon, and we were ready to have some fun!

Blaire's twenty-first birthday was in March, and to fulfill her wish on our daddy-daughter trip years earlier, she, her freshman roommate, Carole, and I were off to Las Vegas.

Conventions had brought me to Vegas many times over the years, but Carole had been only once, and with Blaire hitting a milestone birthday, we decided to go upscale. The limo brought us to the Bellagio, where our penthouse suite, with separate his-and-her bathrooms, overlooked the fountains. Carole was ecstatic.

The crowd had packed Omnia, the luxurious nightclub at Caesar's Palace, when we arrived. When I left the girls to grab beverages at the bar, a gentleman came up to Carole and overlooked the wedding ring on her finger to strike up a spontaneous conversation. For five minutes until I returned, my wife was the queen of the ball!

Blaire asked me later if that brief conversation bothered me.

"Heck no," I replied. "If she played her cards right, he'd have bought the drinks and saved me eighty bucks!"

"CLAY, YOU NEED TO COME GET ME. I fainted," Carole said when she called from her office on a Thursday in June 2018. The next day, our family doctor diagnosed her with general fatigue and sent her home.

"I feel like crap," Carole said that Saturday morning.

"You should probably stay in bed," was my I reply. After all, she'd seen the doctor the day before.

"No, I want to go to the emergency room," she said, and I grabbed my keys.

We sat in the waiting room for forty-five minutes and got no help, so we drove to a drive-up ER in a strip center. With no lines and no waiting, they saw Carole immediately and ran an ultrasound. The doctor walked in thirty minutes later and asked for details about Carole's medical history.

"I strongly suggest you call your oncologist on Monday," he said. "We think we saw something."

"What do you think it was?" I asked.

"It may just be a shadow," he replied, "but take these images to your doctor."

Carole was in surgery again three days later.

"It was about five pounds," Dr. Allen said, describing the tumor he had removed.

"It went from nonexistent to five pounds in six months?" I replied in shock.

"I thought we got it all with the first surgery," he said, "but this one's aggressive."

A week after surgery, we sat in Dr. Allen's conference room as his nurse described the chemotherapy regimen. A cold chill came over me. For the first time in thirty years, despite multiple illnesses, surgeries, and chemotherapies, I realized that Carole might die. It was scary, but I said nothing.

FOR THE FIRST TIME IN THIRTY YEARS,
DESPITE MULTIPLE ILLNESSES, SURGERIES,
AND CHEMOTHERAPIES,
I REALIZED THAT CAROLE MIGHT DIE.

"Hey, we've got a plan, and we're going to knock it out like before," I said with complete confidence as Carole cried on our way home.

Friends frequently chauffeured Carole to Dr. Allen's office for treatment, and soon our lives revolved around the three-week cycle. Carole was fine for two days after treatment, then wiped out for a week. She would slowly come back to normal the second week and have good enthusiasm for the third when it was time to start the process again.

"We're going to make this work," Carole's boss told her. A blended schedule of work-from-home and in-office was perfect because it gave Carole time for treatment and recovery, as well as social stimulation from her coworkers.

Blaire was home that summer, which was a great mental boost for Carole. Offsetting the anguish of her returning cancer was elation over a huge achievement for our oldest daughter. A hospitality major, Blaire applied for the Voyage management training program with Marriott International. She beat out hundreds of other applicants, and four days before returning to Oklahoma State University for her senior year, they offered her a job at the Gaylord Opryland hotel in Nashville, the largest non-gaming hotel in the world. It was a huge load off our minds to know that Blaire had a job lined up a year before she graduated.

"WE'VE BEEN FOLLOWING THE TYPICAL PROTOCOL," Dr. Allen told us four months later after the test results came back. "But we need to change it up."

"I want a second opinion," Carole proclaimed the next day. "MD Anderson is down the street in Houston. I've heard they do miracles, so let's find out!"

"Sounds good to me," I replied. "Let's run it by Dr. Allen and see what he thinks."

"That's a good idea," Allen told us. "In fact, Dr. David, their head of gynecological oncology, is a friend of mine. I'll send the referral, but he consults around the world, and it may be a while before he can see you."

"Dr. David's office called," Carole said the next day. "We have a choice: wait four weeks or they can get us in the day after tomorrow." We packed our bags.

We walked into MD Anderson like we'd walked into St. Peter's Basilica in Rome. It didn't look like a church but had that aura of the mother ship, the central hub for all things cancer.

"Here's what's happening in your body," Dr. David explained in simple terms. He exuded intelligence, which made us think he was likely the smartest person in every room he entered. After an hour of taking us through Ovarian Cancer 101, he said, "What Allen is suggesting is the appropriate protocol. I recommend the same thing."

"Well, that sucked," Carole said as we walked out. "The point of a second opinion from MD Anderson was to get into a clinical trial or try something out of the box, not 'keep-doing-what-you're-doing.' I got screwed."

"It would have been cool if they had something new to try," I replied. "On the other hand, David's opinion is to follow Allen's protocol. It's not as sexy as we hoped, but it is, in fact, a second opinion from MD Anderson."

Carole nodded in agreement. To spice up the trip, we went to a Houston Texans football game that night.

"THE TUMORS APPEAR TO BE SHRINKING!" Dr. Allen told us in early 2019.

That excitement brought fresh wind into Carole's sails at a perfect time. Blaire graduated from college that spring, and we moved her to Nashville to launch her career.

"Once chemo is over, I think we should move," I said to Carole one day. "The kids are all gone, and we never go upstairs anymore. We need something smaller."

It was funny. We'd spent most of our adult lives accumulating lots of things and a big home to put them in, then one day, we wanted to get rid of those things and get a smaller home.

"Where do you want to go?" she asked.

"How about an apartment?" I asked. "A lot of people have made that move and seem to enjoy it. I'm also tired of fixing stuff."

"Okay," she agreed. "Let's see what's out there."

The Star in Frisco, Texas, was a commercial area and headquarters of the Dallas Cowboys football team. Carole and I often went there for dinner, and one evening, I noticed a new building called Twelve. A few clicks on the internet revealed it as an upscale apartment complex.

It was still under construction, so informational appointments were held in an area on the second floor of the Cowboys headquarters. We reviewed the amenities and floor plans, then got to the price.

"That's a healthy number!" I told the sales agent as Carole's eyes grew wide. "So, you're saying this is not a Section 8 housing project, is that right?"

"No, it's not," the agent replied with a smile. "One of the benefits, though, is a membership at the Cowboys Club, the team's private social club," she continued, trying to soften the financial blow. "You still must pay the monthly dues and food and drink, but you go to the top of the waiting list, and we'll waive the initiation fee. The club is right here. Would you like a tour?"

"Sure," Carole and I said together, as we both wanted to see how the Top 2 percent lived.

The club was nice and upscale. Though owned by a football team, it didn't look or feel like a sports bar but more of a members-only lounge in a high-end hotel. It had a bar and restaurant, plus luxurious sitting areas with large-screen TVs, a pool table, and an outdoor patio overlooking the team's practice fields. A separate room and bar called Quarterback Corner had windows to the indoor football field of the Ford Center, where the team practiced and high school teams played some of their games.

"We ain't paying that rent," I laughed on the way home, referring to the apartment complex, "but the club looks interesting. She said the waiting list is about a year. Let's apply and see what happens."

"Go for it," Carole replied, confident this idea would go nowhere. That night I filled out the online application and thought we might hear from them in nine or ten months.

Two days later, my phone rang.

"Mr. Boatright, we got your application. We'd love for you and your wife to come out, tour the club again, and hopefully join us!"

A friend of mine had a son with autism, was married to a former Cowboys player, and was also a member of the club. I mentioned her on the application, and apparently that moved us to the top of the waiting list, along with a nice reduction on the initiation fee.

"Wow, this is nice!" Blaire said as we walked in to sign the paperwork. "Is it expensive?"

"It's not that bad," I replied. "Besides, you're about to graduate and roll off the payroll, so we're going to be flush with cash." Blaire laughed as though I was joking.

Megan, the Membership Director, looked at me and asked, "Are you a Cowboys fan?"

"Of course, but she's the fanatic!" I replied, pointing to Carole. "Last year she was glued to the television for every moment of the NFL Draft." Carole had become a huge football fan and knew more about the players than a professional scout.

We stepped onto the elevator after dinner, and an attractive young couple got on as well, with the gentleman politely nodding hello to each of us. The doors opened in the garage, the couple went their way, and my wife and daughter exploded in hysterics.

"Oh my God, I can't believe that!" they both said at the same time. I looked down to see if a bag of money had been left on the floor.

"What'd I miss?" I asked, obviously clueless.

"That was Leighton Vander Esch!" Carole exclaimed, referring to the Cowboys' star defensive tackle. "You don't know anybody, do you?" she continued, with a combination of laughter and disdain in her voice.

"I know the names but not every player by sight." I defended my ignorance, adding, "His girlfriend was cute. I noticed her!"

A few months later, we signed up for the club's fantasy football draft, a competition neither one of us had done before. On the morning of the draft, we received an email about when and where to meet and that a special surprise was in store.

Our group assembled in the lobby and was led through locked doors to the Cowboys' private suites. Our fantasy football league took place in the Cowboys' actual war room, where owner Jerry Jones and the senior staff executed the real NFL draft every year. I thought Carole was going to have a stroke.

"Okay, this is pretty cool," I said, astounded as well. "Not quite champagne in Buckingham Palace cool, but pretty slick nonetheless!"

The Cowboys Club became our second home, a high-class place where Carole felt pampered. She needed respite from the gloom of cancer and continual changes to her chemo regimen.

SHE NEEDED RESPITE FROM THE GLOOM OF
CANCER AND CONTINUAL CHANGES
TO HER CHEMO REGIMEN.

One night during a conversation with Hailey, a server not much older than Blaire, we mentioned Carole's cancer history. To our surprise, she told us about her chemo treatments as a teenager for Hodgkin's disease, the same cancer Carole had survived almost thirty years earlier. Carole and Hailey formed an immediate bond as the club staff became our extended family.

We became friends with two or three members, but Carole and I knew from day one that this was not our social crowd. That became painfully clear one night after a comedy show in Quarterback Corner with a couple at the table next to us.

"Hi, I'm Carole, and this is my husband, Clay. We live in Plano and have three daughters," my wife said to the wife.

"So do we!" the woman replied with excitement in her voice. They'd recently joined the club and had two daughters the same age as our kids.

"So, what do you do?" the wife asked me. I told her I was in the grocery products business but then made my big mistake. Instead of shutting up, I said I was also an advocate for people with disabilities inspired by our twins. The terrified look on Carole's face indicated that I'd said too much.

"Oh," our new acquaintance responded as her smile fell. At that moment, as though on cue, another woman walked up and sat down at their table with her back to Carole and me.

"Hi, you seem like a lot of fun," she said to the other couple. "My husband and I are with friends over there and would love to have you join us!"

The wife's face perked up as she said, "Oh, thank you!" She grabbed her husband's hand, stood to leave, and said, "It was nice meeting you," while they quickly walked away.

Carole and I sat in dead silence. After a few moments, we got up, left, and didn't say a word on our way home. We never again spoke to someone we didn't know.

"I WANT TO GO TO A COWBOYS THANKSGIVING DAY GAME," Carole had said a hundred times over the years. Like millions of Americans, both our families watched the Thanksgiving games when we were young, and it became a tradition. For twenty years, we'd lived in Dallas, where it was played, but our hellish holidays made attending the game impossible.

"We have tickets on the fifty-yard line!" I told her in October 2019, not revealing what we'd paid. We took the club's private shuttle to the stadium, and though the 'Boys lost to the Buffalo Bills, we were excited to check this event off our bucket list.

On an evening a few weeks before Christmas, Carole attended a wreath-making class at the club while I worked out at the fitness center next door. My cell phone rang in the locker room.

"Clay, this is the reception desk at the Cowboys Club. We need you to come up here." I threw on my shoes and ran out the door.

"She's back in Quarterback Corner," the receptionist said as I got off the elevator. Carole was sitting on a couch with Kassie, one of the club's servers, and Nicholas, a manager, next to her. She looked groggy and incoherent.

"What happened?" I asked, directing the question to anyone who could answer.

"I'm fine. I fainted for a moment," Carole replied as Kassie poured her more water. My wife was the only person I knew who would equate fainting with being fine. She'd been feeling well up to that point, so this caught us off guard. Dr. Allen's office called it a side-effect of the latest chemo regimen and scheduled a new scan for the last week of the year.

MY WIFE WAS THE ONLY PERSON I KNEW
WHO WOULD EQUATE FAINTING WITH BEING FINE.

On Christmas morning, Blaire was in Nashville working through the holidays, and Paige and Mia were in their group home, so Carole and I woke up in an unusually quiet house. For the first time in our lives, we awakened on Christmas without a parent or child at home, which was nice. We brought the twins over for a few hours to celebrate, which made that one of our most enjoyable holidays.

Carole went for her scans a few days later.

We sat in Dr. Allen's exam room in early January and laughed at how well things were going. The holidays had been fun, Blaire was coming home that week, the blood tests showed improvement, and despite her one fainting spell, Carole felt great.

The door opened, and Dr. Allen and his chief nurse walked in. Allen sat down on his chair, looked straight at Carole, and said, "We're still seeing disease progression. I'm sorry, dear, but there's nothing else we can do."

At that moment, Carole's spirit died.

13

FROM MY SIDE TO CHRIST'S SIDE

"I DON'T WANT TO TELL ANYONE," Carole said as we drove home from Dr. Allen's office. For eighteen months, she'd chronicled her treatments, side effects, emotions, and joys on Facebook, but this she wanted to keep private.

The hardest part was not telling Blaire. When she came home a week later to celebrate a late Christmas with us, Carole and I acted as though everything was great and told her about a new cancer trial at UT Southwestern. We didn't tell her the trial was meant to add a few months to her mother's life, not cure the disease.

One of our favorite restaurants was Haywire in Legacy West, an upscale entertainment district in Plano. Carole, Blaire, and I walked in—for what would be Carole's final evening out—and heard a familiar voice call, "Clay . . . Carole!"

Missy was a local civic leader and long-time friend who lived near the restaurant. She told Carole how much she enjoyed her daily Facebook posts and positive attitude and said that she was praying for her. Carole smiled through the silent pain and told Missy she appreciated her comments. We had no idea Missy would be our last friend to see Carole alive.

"Everyone you know is dealing with a crisis you know nothing about, so be kind," was an axiom floating about on social media. As we stood on Haywire's doorstep, that played out to an extreme. In a world where we focus on ourselves, I saw how a spontaneous smile, compliment, and prayer impacted someone who was dying in silence. You may never know when your kindness could be the last thing someone will ever see.

YOU MAY NEVER KNOW WHEN YOUR KINDNESS
COULD BE THE LAST THING SOMEONE
WILL EVER SEE.

Blaire flew back to Nashville, and Carole's deterioration accelerated. She slept twenty hours a day but mustered up enough strength for a trip to UT Southwestern to learn about the life-extending trial.

"I can't die. You wouldn't know how to take care of yourself," Carole had told me for years, only half joking. While I could run a load of clothes, our separation of responsibilities made me ignorant about a lot of things. We sat down at the dining room table one afternoon for the infamous "get your affairs in order" conversation.

"You use your cell phone to deposit checks?" I asked with complete surprise. I thought those ads on television were for people more tech-savvy than us. "How long have you been doing that?"

"About five years," she replied and shook her head in disbelief. "Also, I pay all our bills through my phone, so you'll need to set the accounts up on your cell phone."

"So, we don't write checks anymore?" I continued, scribbling on my notepad. Carole would have stabbed me if a knife had been nearby.

Near the end of January, Carole stopped eating solid food and rarely got out of bed. Her hair was thin and gray, and her skin was dehydrating. The tumor grew unchecked and made her appear seven months pregnant.

"Find Dr. Davis and tell him we need to speak as soon as possible," I instructed the nurse when I called the head of the life-extending trial. Carole had not eaten or walked out of the bedroom in days, and she looked ninety years old. If she was going to participate in a trial, it had to be soon.

CAROLE HAD NOT EATEN OR WALKED OUT
OF THE BEDROOM IN DAYS, AND SHE
LOOKED NINETY YEARS OLD.

An hour later, Dr. Davis called from an out-of-town conference. I described Carole's condition and asked him what to do.

"Carole knows she's dying," he replied. "Her body is turning itself off, and her mind is coming to terms with that. She won't make it to the trial. Let me refer you to hospice."

It felt like the temperature in the room had dropped fifty degrees. I walked into our bedroom with no idea what to say.

"Hi, sweetheart. Are you awake?" I asked and sat on the edge of the bed.

"Yes," she replied in a quiet voice.

"I spoke with Dr. Davis. He doesn't think the trial will work and suggested they call hospice. Do you want him to call them?" I asked, confident she knew the ramifications of her answer.

"Yes," she responded without hesitation.

167

It was Thursday, February 6, 2020. I called Dr. Davis back and then called Blaire in Nashville.

"Mom's not doing well, and hospice is coming out," I told her. "You were here last week, but you might want to come back in the next week or so to see her."

We thought it would be okay for Blaire to wait a few days, but Amanda, Blaire's apartment roommate, told her to go home right away. Amanda's mother had passed away years earlier and knew there was no benefit to waiting.

Carole got a surprise burst of energy when she learned Blaire was on her way. She sat on the couch, alert and engaged for the first time in weeks when we spoke with the hospice rep the next day. She even laughed a few times. Carole confirmed the services she wanted, and a nurse came out that afternoon. The nurse walked me through a host of pain-relieving drugs, both liquid and tablet, and described with precision when to give what and why.

Blaire and her boyfriend, Trevor, spent the weekend by her mother's side. Trevor took Blaire to the airport late Sunday afternoon, but before they left, we worked out a plan. If the time arrived during the day, I would first call Bakah, Blaire's best friend at work. If at night, I would call Amanda, her roommate. The second call would be to Trevor, and the third to Blaire. We wanted Blaire's support network ready when she learned that her mother had died.

At 9:45 p.m. on Monday night, I was watching television in the family room when Carole walked out of our bedroom. I helped her to the couch and asked how she felt but got no response. She hadn't eaten in a week, so I retrieved some gelatin from the fridge and hoped to get something in her system.

I fed my wife Jell-O on our sofa and whispered, "I love you" into her ear. She murmured it back, almost inaudible. Then suddenly, out of nowhere, came an overwhelming sensation I'd never experienced.

Love was the first thing that came to mind, but it was amplified over a hundred times and erupting in a single moment. It confirmed I was exactly where I needed to be. Later, it became clear the Holy Spirit was wrapping His arms around us.

After a few minutes, I helped Carole back to bed. It was getting late, so I changed clothes and joined her. The deep rasp she took with each breath was unbearable to hear.

"Dear God, You have the power to heal her in an instant and restore Carole in the blink of an eye. You also have the power to bring her home to You. Whichever You decide, please do it now," I prayed as I fell asleep.

Around 2:00 a.m., I opened my eyes and saw Carole standing in the corner of our bedroom, seeming to stare at a picture of her late mother on our bookshelf. Not knowing what she needed, I jumped up to help.

"Do you need to go to the bathroom?" I asked. "Or do you want to go back to bed?"

Carole slowly walked to the bed and tried to lie perpendicular across it. I gently turned her body in the right direction and pulled up the covers.

Her breath smelled horrible. Carole was very particular about oral hygiene, so I stepped into our bathroom and put toothpaste on my finger to brush her teeth as one would a baby. I returned to the bed, lifted her head, and gently opened her mouth.

At that moment, alone in silent darkness, Jesus brought my wife of thirty years from my side to His side. I cradled Carole in my hands as tears ran down my face. I leaned over, gave her a kiss on the cheek, and said, "I love you, baby girl."

AT THAT MOMENT, ALONE IN SILENT DARKNESS, JESUS BROUGHT MY WIFE OF THIRTY YEARS FROM MY SIDE TO HIS SIDE.

The room was pitch black and incredibly quiet—dead silence.

What do I do now? I asked myself. The hospice people never shared a plan if Carole passed away at night, so I called the number on the back of their brochure.

"I think my wife died," I told the answering service.

"I'm really busy right now," the operator replied. "Can I put you on hold?"

"Lady, that's the wrong answer!" I shouted as my heart raced, and I hung up the phone.

If someone dies, I guess you call 9-1-1, was my next thought. The dispatcher told me to turn on the porch lights for the police and paramedics. I called the hospice number again, told the operator what happened, and she said a nurse would be sent to the house immediately.

"It's a little late for that now," I told her. Later, I realized the nurse was not coming to take care of Carole but to get the drugs from our home.

"If your wife is on hospice, you shouldn't have to call us," the paramedic said as they and the police came in the front door.

"Nobody ever told me that," I replied. "I'm also not a physician. I thought she was gone, but I wasn't totally sure. That's why I called you."

We walked to the bedroom, and one of the police officers asked for Carole's driver's license. I pulled the card out of her purse and handed it over.

"Mr. Boatright, please sit here for a few minutes," the police officer said as she escorted me to the family room. From their standpoint, this house was a potential crime scene. All the police knew was someone had made a 9-1-1 call, and they showed up and found a dead body in the bedroom. Some guy claiming to be her husband said she supposedly died of cancer.

"Are you sure this is your wife's driver's license?" the officer asked when she returned a minute later.

"Yes, it is," I answered.

"Are you sure?" she asked again.

"Miss, I was married to my wife for thirty years. I know what her driver's license looks like," I said, annoyed and curious about why this was an issue.

The officer sensed my emotion and calmly explained, "I'm sorry I had to ask, but she doesn't look like the picture. We need to make sure for the identification. Can you confirm that it is Carole Boatright?"

"Yes," I replied, as tears started to flow again.

"Would you like for us to call a chaplain?" the second officer asked.

"No, I appreciate it, but I'm fine," I told him. A few more minutes went by, and his partner asked again.

"Thanks, but I know more preachers than you can shake a stick at," I replied with a smile.

When they asked a third time, I laughed and gave in with, "Apparently y'all think I need a chaplain. Okay, let's wake up somebody's ass in the middle of the night to come over here in the cold and tell me I'm going to be okay!"

The police chaplain, funeral home team, and hospice nurse showed up around 4:30 a.m. The nurse disposed of the remaining morphine while the funeral home guys waited for the police crime scene photographer to finish taking pictures. Meanwhile, Pastor Bob and I started to chat.

"I feel bad about getting you out on a cold morning," I told him, "but everyone seemed to think I need to talk to somebody, so it's your lucky day!"

We sat at the dining room table while a half-dozen people scurried around the kitchen and bedroom. When I finished walking Pastor Bob through our crazy family history, he said something I'll never forget.

"You and Carole did something which, sadly, is rare these days," he observed. "You actually fulfilled your wedding vows, until death do you part."

I thanked him for saying that, though it seemed odd to be proud of not getting a divorce. We were special needs parents, where the divorce rate was rumored to be 80 percent, and we could make each other crazy, but there was no way Carole could make me so mad that I would abandon my family.

"YOU AND CAROLE DID SOMETHING WHICH, SADLY, IS RARE THESE DAYS," HE OBSERVED. "YOU ACTUALLY FULFILLED YOUR WEDDING VOWS, UNTIL DEATH DO YOU PART."

"Clay, you seem to be handling things well. How do you deal with the stress?" he asked.

"I'm the king of compartmentalization," I replied. "Put it in a box, put the box on a shelf, pull it out when needed. Having raised three children, two with severe disabilities, and Carole's first cancer in our mid-twenties and now eighteen months of this, I've learned to take things in stride."

"That's an admirable skill," said Pastor Bob. "Most people don't handle it that well." I appreciated his comment but wasn't sure if he was sincere or trying to be nice.

"I also never look backward," I responded. "Carole's gone, and there's nothing I can do about it. What I must do now is focus on the future."

I took a long pause. "I'd like your thoughts on something," I continued. "I've known all along that there was a chance Carole could die, and I've been preparing for the last month. The one element I haven't figured out is how to tell Paige and Mia, the two people who won't understand that their mother has passed away. For weeks, I've cried every time I think about it, and I don't know what to do."

Pastor Bob paused for a second and asked, "You said they moved into their own home a couple of years ago, right?"

"Yes, sir," I confirmed.

"Well, maybe put it in terms they can relate to. You can tell them, 'Mom has moved to a new house. We won't see her for a while, but someday in the future, we'll move there with her, and we'll all be together.'" My eyes teared up as he spoke.

The funeral home team rolled the gurney toward the front door around 6:00 a.m. Pastor Bob stopped them in the entry hall and asked if he could say a prayer. He thanked God for Carole, our marriage and family, citing each person by name. When he left that morning at 7:30, the last person out the door, I told Pastor Bob that I appreciated him being there. From now on, if the police ever suggest I call a chaplain, I'll call a chaplain.

Blaire's flight arrived later that day. We decided not to tell anyone that Carole had passed until after we told Mia and Paige. While we drove to the twins' house, I told Blaire Pastor Bob's suggestion, and she replied, "Daddy, I'm their sister. Let me tell them."

Blaire knelt on the floor in front of her sisters and told them that their Mom had moved away. I watched from across the room, and again my eyes started to sweat.

My parents were buried in a town where none of us lived, in a cemetery we never visited. Carole's mother and father, meanwhile, were in our guest room in cremation urns. Carole and I agreed that we wanted that for ourselves, too. As the funeral home wheeled Carole out, they asked if they should proceed with the cremation.

I started to say yes, but then said, "No, Blaire may want to see her mom one last time."

BLAIRE AND I WALKED INTO THE FUNERAL HOME two days later. The last time I'd seen Carole was in the chaos of our house, and I wanted to say goodbye in private. I asked Blaire to stay back for a few moments.

The funeral home director escorted me to the bier, and as he pulled back the sheet, a calm relief came over me. Unlike two days earlier, when Carole looked so old that the police couldn't identify her, she looked like her fifty-four-year-old self, appearing sound asleep as though she'd never been sick.

The director said we could stay as long as we wished. I held Carole's hand, looked at her beautiful face, and felt grateful for a final memory I hadn't anticipated. After a few minutes, Blaire walked up, and I left her alone with her mom for their private moment.

"I WANT TO HAVE A CELEBRATION OF LIFE at the Cowboys Club, officiated by Ron, and I want a lot of people to show up," Carole said at our get-your-affairs-in-order conversation a few weeks earlier. Renting Quarterback Corner at the club was easy, and Ron, a pastor from Prestonwood, would surely officiate—but I couldn't guarantee the attendance.

"Clay, let us know what you need," said Stacy, the club's general manager, in an email the day after Carole passed. I emailed her back and asked about the fee to rent QBC for the celebration. She replied that they would take care of it.

Our family walked in an hour before the start time and was amazed by what we saw. The club created an altar in front of the windows that overlooked the indoor football field, while pictures of Carole, pulled from her Facebook page, looped on the monitors. Tea, water, and hors d'oeuvres were on the tables, all a gift from the club.

A hundred and twenty-five people heard speakers from each area of Carole's life. My sister spoke about family, while Blaire's college roommate shared how Carole was a second mother to many of their friends. A fellow drill team mom discussed the life of dance moms, and our former Bible study leader talked about Carole's faith in God.

Dacia, one of Carole's closest work friends, surprised everyone the most. She was initially reluctant to speak but ultimately agreed. With a dry, subtle sense of humor, she used stories of their work antics to lighten the room and put smiles on everyone's faces. Those who paid close attention learned that Dacia was gay and a long-term cancer patient going through chemotherapy at that moment.

It could not have been more appropriate that Carole's final wish was fulfilled with an evangelical Christian service in a private bar, overlooking a professional football field, with laughs from a seriously ill, bald lesbian.

"THIS IS STARTING TO GET WEIRD," I told Blaire as we looked at three boxes of ashes—Carole and her parents—from a cremation tower in our guest room. Carole wanted her ashes to be sprinkled in Old Hickory Lake near my sister's Nashville lake house, a place she loved to visit and relax. Blaire and I decided that on Easter, a mass sprinkle with ashes of all three would be a fitting final ceremony.

Our family floated offshore on a pontoon boat with the ashes on board. I thanked God for Carole's parents as we poured their ashes into the water. After another prayer for Carole, my brother-in-law fired up the engine and sped across the lake while I poured Carole's ashes behind us. Because ash is lighter than water, they floated on top and looked like an airplane vapor trail that stretched a hundred yards behind the boat.

"I've always wanted to live in the Jeannie bottle," Carole said a million times, referring to *I Dream of Jeannie*, her favorite TV show as a child.

AFTER ANOTHER PRAYER FOR CAROLE,
MY BROTHER-IN-LAW FIRED UP THE ENGINE
AND SPED ACROSS THE LAKE WHILE I POURED
CAROLE'S ASHES BEHIND US.

On Christmas, a decade before she passed, I'd given Carole a 1964 Jim Beam whiskey bourbon decanter, the prop used as the Jeannie bottle on the show. Carole was skilled in crafts and hand-painted it as an exact replica of the original TV version, which we displayed in our bedroom.

Before we left for Nashville, I found two of Carole's lipstick cases, cleaned them out, and brought them on the boat. Before pouring Carole into the lake, I filled both tubes with her ashes. Returning home, I put the ash-filled lipstick cases in that Christmas present, enabling Carole to fulfill her dream of living forever in the Jeannie bottle.

ONE AFTERNOON I OPENED A DRAWER on Carole's nightstand and found a small pink album. It was handmade with Carole's calligraphy and creativity. The written words told a story, while the photos and hand-drawn pictures complemented the narrative. I read it and started to cry. I could hear Carole's voice as though she was sharing her own eulogy. The title page said Once Upon a Time.

Once upon a time, there was a little family in Plano—The Boatrights. Carole & Clay were the dad & mom. Blaire was their daughter. They were happy but wanted to have another baby, and God blessed them with identical twin daughters. They were happy, but they were tired!

Carole was worried about the babies, Paige and Mia. Mia bobbed her head constantly. Paige had to rock all the time. The girls were not meeting their milestones. They did not talk. So, Carole & Clay took the girls to all sorts of doctors.

"They're preemies; they'll catch up!" "Some kids just do that," and *"It's OK, Mom, the girls will be all right!" are what they heard.*

Finally, the Boatrights got an answer to what was going on with their precious little girls. It was <u>not</u> what they wanted to hear!

The next page of the book showed a mass of black and red streaks, implying pain, fear, and death. On the opposite page, a small clipping read, *I have autism.* I turned the page again and saw a collage of words:

What? It's not fair! No! Why Us, God? Not our girls! No! How can we do this?

Well, Clay seemed to accept the twins' disabilities quicker than Carole. Carole was MAD! She resented all the demands the twins put on their lives. She was jealous that their family was not the typical Plano family. Carole was tired! She was frustrated that she didn't know what to do to help Paige & Mia. God must be punishing the Boatrights for something they have done, reasoned Carole.

But Carole was not listening to the small voice of GOD talking to her. (Well, actually, it wasn't a small voice, but when you are angry, it is easy to put God on the back burner.) GOD SAID:

I know what you are thinking. You need a sign. And you would like that sign to be complete healing for Paige and Mia. I could do that, but I will not. I am not your cosmic vending machine. I have given you a gift that you do not recognize yet. I am giving you the opportunity to grow in me while raising your special children. You will unwrap this gift all the days of your life. It will not be easy, but I will BE THERE. This gift will not only be for you and Clay. Others will help with the unwrapping. They may question why they received it. My ways are not your ways, but I am God, and I love Paige, Mia, & You!

I closed the book and held it for a long time to cherish Carole's last words.

14

GOD IN THE GROCERY STORE

VALENTINE'S DAY CAME THREE DAYS after Carole died, and for the first time in thirty-three years, I was alone on the evening meant for couples. Cloaked in sadness as I walked into the Tom Thumb grocery, the future was bleak. My best friend—my only friend—was gone.

I sulked through the store feeling sorry for myself, then stopped dead in my tracks in the haircare aisle. I froze in place as my mind and emotions suddenly uplifted! In an instant, God revealed two things with absolute clarity.

First, Carole was doing *great*, far better than the rest of us! No longer in pain, she was worshiping at the throne of God, which is exactly what we Christians strive for. God released me from mourning my wife, as we don't mourn someone experiencing God in all His Glory. After Carole died, many people thought I should live in sadness over her death. I never will because Carole's faith in Jesus Christ took care of that.

God also reframed my future. I was married for thirty years and, at fifty-five, hopefully had another thirty or more ahead of me. In other words, I wasn't even halfway finished! With Carole in Heaven and our children out of the house, for the first time in my life, I had virtually no obligations or responsibilities. Heck, I was barely responsible for myself and could do whatever I wanted. That was a unique opportunity. So, standing in aisle 9 of Tom Thumb on Valentine's Day, I launched Clay 2.0. The million-dollar question was, "What does God want me to do with this opportunity?"

Despite my Valentine's Day revelation, sneak attacks occurred a few times, always at the most unexpected moment. A couple of weeks after Carole's passing, I drove to a local café for breakfast. It was a few blocks from our home, and Carole and I had often walked there on Saturday mornings.

Our favorite booth in the corner by the windows was open. I glanced at the menu, like many times before, lowered it, and was hit by an emotional tsunami. I looked across the table, and no one was there. Carole would sit in that spot, stir her coffee, and talk about our plans for the day. Instead, there was only an empty seat.

I held it together through the eggs and bacon, made it back to the car, and cried like a baby for ten minutes. The emotional release was painful, but it cleansed my system to move forward.

Life has a way of rejuvenating for the long term. A fire destroys the forest, and soon a sapling sprouts up in the carnage. Families also have life cycles; when one era ends, another begins.

"HI, CLAY. DO YOU HAVE DINNER PLANS FOR TONIGHT?" Trevor asked a few weeks after Carole died. I had known Blaire's boyfriend for a few years and liked him, but he'd never asked me out to dinner.

"I'm open," I replied, surprised and suspicious that something was up.

Trevor arrived first and was already working on a drink when I sat down at our table. After a few routine niceties, he handed me a box that contained a lovely engagement ring.

"I talked to my mother and father this morning and want to let you know," he started. "When Blaire comes back to town next week, I'm going to ask her to marry me." He was telling me, not asking me, which I respected. They were both adults and didn't need my permission.

"The ring is beautiful," I said as I handed the box back to him. "Trevor, I have a question. What is your goal for dinner tonight? Is it for me to say, 'Oh, this is great news, I'm so excited,' or is it to have a conversation?" My voice deepened to a serious level.

"Umm, to have a conversation," Trevor replied.

I leaned forward, looked the young man in the eye, and said, "Well, buckle up."

I didn't want to grill him or tell him what to do, but I wanted to understand his thoughts. His response to the first question caught my attention.

"Trevor, you're a good-looking guy. You're smart, you're the life of the party, and you work your ass off. You could have your pick of the litter when it comes to women," I told him.

Then came the surprise question.

"Why do you want to marry Blaire? I've adored her since the moment she was born and think she's great, but she's also a little high maintenance with her own host of idiosyncrasies. Why her?"

If he offered a knee-jerk response like "I love her," I was going to say, "Well, you love your dog too. Are you going to marry it?" He didn't go there.

"No matter where I am or what I'm doing," he replied, "it's always better when Blaire is with me."

That answer made me take a long pause. For over three decades, that's what I'd said about Carole.

We talked for two hours and covered work-life balance, divorce, having kids, having special needs kids, and living on one income. We also discussed religion.

"I don't think you have to go to church every Sunday to be a Christian," Trevor said to his future father-in-law, a guy who drove his family to church every Sunday.

"I agree," I replied. "Sitting in a church doesn't make you a Christian any more than sitting in a garage makes you a car. What God wants more than anything is for us to develop a relationship with Him. How did you develop your relationship with Blaire? You learned about her, what she liked, and what she needed. The same is true with God. Church and Bible study provide information about God to develop a relationship. I'm not going to tell you what to do, but as time goes on, it's something to think about."

Trevor nodded as he realized that unsolicited advice from the father-in-law came with the wedding package. More importantly, I owed it to Carole to share how we had fulfilled our wedding vows.

EVEN IN OUR DARKEST MOMENTS, GOD WAS WITH US.

Even in our darkest moments, God was with us. Over the years, I had twice been laid off from my job, borrowed money to pay our bills, and raised three children, including two with severe disabilities who couldn't speak and had harmful behaviors. I'd been screamed at by my wife, supported her and our daughters through multiple life-threatening illnesses, and ultimately held Carole's head in my hands, alone in silent darkness, as I watched her die in our bed.

In the face of those challenges, God worried about nothing, so neither did I. Eventually, I became financially secure, my children experienced their best lives possible, and our futures were bright. While none of those were deserved, but solely through God's grace, my compass always centered on three things: 1) trust God during the most difficult times, 2) always appreciate what I have, and 3) never *ever* abandon my family.

15

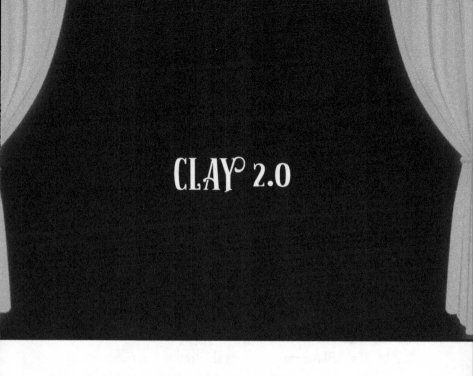

CLAY 2.0

THE DAY AFTER CAROLE'S CELEBRATION OF LIFE, my brother, sister, and I sat around my dining room table.

"Clay," my brother Jeff said, "for over thirty years, you've been taking care of somebody. Carole's illnesses, Blaire, the twins and their challenges. Now, for the first time in your adult life, you don't have anybody to care for. Can you handle that?"

The question made me pause.

"That's an outstanding question," I said. "I don't know."

A few days earlier, in Tom Thumb, God had pointed out that I didn't have any responsibilities, but not being needed by anyone could be difficult. One thing was for sure: if I wanted a future, I had to seize it.

It's been said that there's a reason why our windshield is large and our rearview mirror is small. It's because what's in front of us is significantly more important than what's behind us. Focusing on the road ahead is what got me through life's challenges. To enjoy the journey, I would have to leave the five-bedroom house where we raised our children and where Carole died.

"When I was your age, I wanted to live in Manhattan," I told Blaire a few days after Carole passed. "The lights, the hustle and bustle of people, and walking to restaurants in the neighborhood. I'm not moving to New York, but let's go check out Legacy West."

We sat down with the leasing agent and gave him my wish list: two bedrooms (one for an office), a front door that didn't open into the kitchen (for a more homey feel), and a balcony that overlooked the main street (to maximize the Manhattan-like experience). There were six apartments in the 620-unit complex that met those criteria, and one had recently become available.

"Daddy!" Blaire exclaimed as she stepped out onto the balcony. "This is the perfect apartment for you now that Mom is gone. It's right across the street from Victoria's Secret!"

"That's outstanding!" I said and burst out laughing. "The best part is that no one would have appreciated that more than your mother!" The next day, I signed the lease on what I called the Corner Suite.

"This is pretty cool," Blaire said a month later as we ate hamburgers and watched people and traffic below the apartment balcony. Bellagio-style fountains under us were a popular spot where professional photographers helped models expand their portfolios and parents snapped pictures of their kids by the water.

"Between Victoria's Secret and the Lamborghinis, the view's not bad!" I replied as a bright green Lambo drove by at a snail's pace. A McLaren and Ferrari followed not far behind.

"Okay, that's weird," I said four minutes later. "There's the green Lamborghini again coming the other way. He didn't have time to stop and do anything." That's when it hit me.

The exotic cars were cruising up and down the strip to see and be seen.

A MORNING WALK BECAME MY DAILY RITUAL. A stroll through Legacy West after sunrise was like walking down Bourbon Street in New Orleans in the early morning but without the stink.

"Hi. Excuse me," I heard a woman say as she walked up behind me. She was in her early thirties, possibly of Filipino descent, and wore large, dark sunglasses.

"The Bible verse on your shirt means a lot to me today," she said.

I looked down to remember what shirt I was wearing. It had Jeremiah 29:11 imprinted on the back. *"For I know the plans I have for you,"* declares the Lord, *"plans to prosper you and not to harm you, plans to give you hope and a future."*

"I'm so glad," I replied, then paused for a moment. "If you don't mind me asking, is there something difficult going on in your life right now?"

"Yes," she answered, as a big tear rolled down her cheek. "My husband was diagnosed with cancer and won't survive. We got away from the kids this weekend to stay at the Renaissance to say goodbye."

"I'm so sorry. What type of cancer does he have?" I asked.

"Liver."

"How old is he?"

"Thirty-four."

"I know what you're going through," I told her. "My wife passed away from ovarian cancer a year ago."

"Oh, I'm sorry!" she replied with shock on her face.

"Thanks, but it's all good!" I said with a smile. "A few days after she passed, God helped me see that Carole is doing great, experiencing what all Christians aspire to! I don't have to mourn her. Is your husband a believer?"

"Yes," she said, nodding her head, "but that doesn't make it easier for me!"

Another tear fell from behind her glasses.

"I totally understand," I said. "How old are your kids?"

She put her hand down low, indicating that her children were small.

"My prayer for you," I continued, "is what God shared with me. You're young and have many years ahead, and there are great opportunities out there for you to seize. It's going to be tough, particularly with your kids, but you will get through it."

"Thank you!" she replied, as a smile came to her face.

"Certainly! May I ask, what is your husband's name?"

"Brian, and my name is Christian," she answered, with her smile growing bigger.

I asked one more question. "May I say a prayer right now?"

"Yes, thank you," Christian affirmed.

"Oh, Heavenly Father," I said as we bowed our heads, "we love You so much. Thank You for Brian and Christian, the love they have for each other and their family. It's tough right now, so we ask that You put Your loving arms around them and be with Brian as he comes to spend eternity with You. Please be with Christian and the children as they start the new path You have for them. We know it will be magnificent, and we thank You for that. In Your Son's name, we pray, Amen."

"Thank you so much!" Christian said as she turned and walked toward the hotel.

I continued my stroll.

WHILE THE CORNER SUITE WAS FUN, I soon found myself living the old expression, "The loneliest place in the world is in the middle of a crowded room." On many nights, I'd people-watch from the balcony over the fountains. It didn't take long to realize that almost everyone below was paired up or out with friends or family. This discovery highlighted the most painful part of losing my only friend, the loneliness.

The pain was stark, with the worst occurring on one of the best days of my life.

. . . I SOON FOUND MYSELF LIVING THE OLD EXPRESSION, "THE LONELIEST PLACE IN THE WORLD IS IN THE MIDDLE OF A CROWDED ROOM."

Blaire and Trevor married a year after Carole died. Before I walked Blaire down the aisle, I brought in a bouquet of fall flowers, Carole's favorite, and placed them on a chair draped in white in the front row. I walked back up the aisle.

Blaire made it clear from day one that she wanted her sisters at her wedding. Karmen brought Paige and Mia to the venue a few minutes before the ceremony and kept them in the reception hall with Blaire, so no one knew they were there.

After I placed Carole's bouquet and returned, I put my arm around Mia. With Louis Armstrong's "It's a Wonderful World" in the background, she and I walked down the aisle, one small step after another.

Mia sat next to Karmen in the front row, and I returned for Paige and walked her down next. I knelt next to the twins, said, "I love you," and gave them a kiss before I retrieved the bride. It's not unusual for a man with three daughters to walk each down the wedding aisle. But it's rare to do it on the same day.

The quick ceremony was followed by a fried chicken dinner and hours of dancing. A few minutes past midnight, everyone was gone, and I climbed into the only car left in the dark parking lot. The engine started, and a cold chill engulfed me.

Over 170 people, most of whom I didn't know, had left my party with someone else. Meanwhile, here I was—the host—all alone. The same dead silence from the night Carole died surrounded me again. I wanted to cry but was frozen in my seat. Carole was supposed to be sitting next to me, dammit, on the day she and I had dreamed about for years. The pain was excruciating. I drove home to the Corner Suite, unpacked the car, and sat in the dark for the rest of the night.

"I'm NOT LETTING A STRANGER come into my apartment!" the attractive young woman said to the delivery guy as I walked by her door. Curious, I stopped and turned toward them, close enough to engage if needed. The delivery dude saw me, said something in Spanish, and walked away.

"Hi. My name is Clay. I live in the apartment at the end of the hall," I said to my brunette neighbor in a tight sweatshirt and leggings. "If you ever need anything, please let me know."

"Thank you so much for stopping. You are so sweet," she replied, as I continued to the garage.

Around 10:30 that night, I heard a knock on my door. I opened it, and to my surprise, there stood the sweatshirt and leggings.

"Hi, Clay. You seem like a really nice guy," she said. "Would you like to come to my apartment and have a drink?"

At that moment, every ounce of my fifty-five-year-old, out-of-shape, non-drinking Christian dad bod knew the right answer was, *I appreciate it, but it's late, and I need to pass.*

"Uh, sure. Let me get my shoes," I said instead, and followed the athletic, twenty-seven-year-old nurse down the hallway. I returned to my apartment at nine the next morning after a few hours of sleep. *Well, at least she was older than Blaire,* I rationalized to myself.

THE COWBOYS CLUB WAS MY PAIN-FREE OASIS after Carole's death. I lived and worked alone in my apartment, so aside from my daughters, the club staff were the only people I saw on a regular basis. Booth 514 at the back of the bar became command central for the transition to Clay 2.0.

"John, I need to tap your expertise," I said to the club's sommelier one night.

"Go for it, boss. How can I help?" he replied as he sat down.

"I'm fifty-five years old," I said, "and have never found an adult beverage I like. It's no big deal, but ordering a Diet Coke all the time has gotten old. It may be due to my warped palette."

"What's wrong with your palette?" he asked.

"Years ago, I found out that I can't taste anything sour," I answered. "It doesn't register on my tongue at all."

"Interesting," he observed. "I'm guessing red wine doesn't do much for you."

My jaw dropped. "How did you know that?" I asked. "A five-dollar bottle and a five-hundred-dollar bottle both taste the same to me, like warm grape juice."

"If you can't taste sour, that means you can't taste acid," John explained. "It's the acid that gives red wine its unique flavor." In thirty seconds, John answered a decades-long question.

"Can you help me find a cocktail that doesn't taste like swamp water or cotton candy?" I pleaded, back to the original challenge.

"I'll be right back," he said as he got up and walked away. Three minutes later, John returned with a glass on a tray.

"Here, try this," he offered.

There was no fragrance when it passed my nose, and a mild flavor as it poured over my tongue and down my throat. I followed with a second sip.

"That's not bad," I said, relieved that it wasn't horrible but also underwhelmed. "What is it?"

"That's a vanilla vodka and Pepsi," John said, happy that I didn't throw up.

"Well, that explains why it tastes like a Vanilla Coke," I replied and paused for several seconds. "Question," I said, laughing. "Would a man with my obvious testosterone order this with a group of guys at a bar?"

"I think people should order whatever they like," John replied, "but I see your point. I'll be right back."

Three minutes later, he returned with another glass on a tray. "Here, try this," he instructed again.

A single ice cube was immersed in a light brown beverage with an orange peel and cherry. I took a sip.

"Ooh, now we're talking!" I exclaimed. The drink had a mild kick and a nice array of flavors that I could nurse for a couple of hours. "What is it?" I asked.

"That, my friend, is an Old Fashioned, and you can order it anywhere in the world, and nobody will think about it twice," John replied, successfully meeting the challenge at hand.

My JUNIOR HIGH SCHOOL was several miles from our house when I was growing up, so my parents gave me a red Honda motorcycle to ride until I turned sixteen. Carole would have ripped my lungs out if I'd suggested getting one after we got married, but now, with no responsibilities, I shopped around. I soon learned a motorcycle driver's license was required to even go for a test ride.

The porch of the motorcycle dealership had a variety of bikes and other machines, including one that looked like a cool 1920s British race car. It rode like an automobile but had no doors or roof and only three wheels, two in front and one in back.

"What is it?" I asked the sales rep.

"It's called a Vanderhall," he replied. "They're made in Utah. The state considers it a motorcycle, but you don't need a cycle license. Give it a test drive."

Five minutes into the drive, I was bitten, and I ordered one the next day. It was unique, flashy, and became the center of attention at every stoplight.

A few months later, I was inspired by the green Lamborghini and cruised the strip in front of the Corner Suite when a gentleman crossed in front. It was common for people to stare when the Vanderhall drove by.

"Very nice!" he said with a smile and big thumbs-up.

"Thanks!" I shouted back. "This is our second date!" I didn't know if he was referring to the Vanderhall or the attractive blonde next to me. Maybe both.

"DADDY, WE NEED TO BUY YOU SOME NEW CLOTHES," Blaire said with a smile.

"What brought this on?" I asked.

"You have holes in your shirt," she replied.

"Am I embarrassing you?" I inquired, curious about her sudden interest in my wardrobe.

"No, but you're not poor," she answered with an assumption that she was not qualified to make.

"I'm familiar with my net worth," I assured her.

"Then we're getting you some nice shirts to wear!" she said with conviction.

"I'm not poor because I don't buy shirts I don't need!"

"We're also going through your closet and throwing out every shirt older than me!" she continued.

"Well heck, I won't have anything to wear!"

"Clay 2.0 . . . ya gotta look the part!" My advisor refused to take no for an answer.

Bashar was a men's fashion consultant and fellow member of the Cowboys Club.

"My friend, you're an artist, and this is a canvas," I said as I pointed to my body. "This canvas needs help!" He smiled in silent agreement.

A week later, Bashar and his tailor visited the Corner Suite and measured every part and appendage on my body. The new sports coats, pants, and shirts arrived a month—and several thousand dollars—later. They looked good and felt great because for the first time in my life I had clothes that fit!

A cool apartment across from Victoria's Secret, a flashy car, a classic beverage, and a new wardrobe. Clay 2.0 was up and running!

16

THE FINAL CHAPTER

"I WANT YOU TO BE A WOLF," she said in her heavy Russian accent one night on my couch in the Corner Suite.

That's when I realized that dating had changed a lot since Pizza Hut in 1986.

A few months earlier, I was living in a nondescript suburban home, watching television every night with my empty-nest wife, and my excitement was eating catfish blackened instead of fried. Now, less than a year later, I was a widower in an apartment thirty feet above an entertainment district with a five-foot divorced Muscovite who wanted me to—well, that was to be determined. Yeah, dating in my mid-fifties was going to be a different experience!

CHURCH! I THOUGHT TO MYSELF. That would be a great place to meet a new companion and, more important, reengage in the faith. Several singles fellowships for my age group met at a local megachurch, so over two weekends, I visited seven of them.

"These people are half dead but don't know it yet," I told a pastor friend a few weeks later. The class members were nice, but their lack of energy was painful.

"Maybe you should try some younger classes," he suggested. That seemed like a good idea since my enthusiasm and outlook on life aligned more with the forty-year-olds than the fifty-five-plus crowd. I emailed the church director of those classes for his advice.

"I'm not sure our groups would be right for you," he replied. "However, our church has a wonderful grief recovery class you should consider."

This was a far cry from the *We'd love to have you* response I expected from my Christian brother. I sent him a nice note:

Thanks, Dave. I appreciate you getting back to me. You and I obviously haven't met, otherwise you'd know that I'm the end objective of the grief recovery class!

"Please join us," John and Jane said as we walked into the restaurant. We were close in age, had met a few weeks earlier, and ran into each other again on our way to lunch.

"What are you looking for?" Jane asked when I said dating was something I was considering.

"I'm not looking to get married again," I answered with a smile. "I made one woman's life miserable for decades, and no one else should endure that again! A new long-term partner, however, would be nice."

"We often meet people and can keep an eye out for you," Jane offered. She took a long look at her husband, then back to me.

"You should know we're in the lifestyle."

Hello! My monogamous marriage didn't make me totally ignorant. "The lifestyle" was the modern term for "swingers." The wolf conversation started to sound normal.

"Really?" I said calmly, as though she had said her favorite color was blue. "That's interesting. So how did that come about?"

"YOU SHOULD KNOW WE'RE IN THE LIFESTYLE."

I had no idea where the conversation was going, but the trip could be interesting.

"We've been married almost thirty years too," she continued, "and with the kids out of the house, we got bored. We heard about Club Collette in Dallas, where couples go to meet, so we gave it a try."

"Do your family and friends know?" I asked.

"No," she said. "In fact, you're the first person outside the lifestyle that we've mentioned it to."

I appreciated her confidence. People often felt comfortable talking to me because I treated everyone with respect and wasn't judgmental. However, my challenge in this conversation was to keep from laughing.

"So, do you meet people at Collette and hook up?" I inquired as I took a bite of my cheeseburger.

"We met a couple at the club, and they've become our regular go-to friends," John explained, along with details on the special room in their home with cameras for private viewing.

Over the next two hours, I learned more about their sex life than I knew about my own. At the end, I thought Carole had died and left me on Mars.

CAROLE AND I HAD LOTS OF ACQUAINTANCES but not many close friends, so nobody lined up to hang out with a widower. A couple of people asked me to lunch after Carole died, but nothing more. Eating alone every night wasn't fun, so I had an idea.

"Guess what I did," I laughed on the call to Blaire.

She paused for a moment and replied with intuition, "You signed up for Christian Mingle?!"

"Yes, I did. With a profile and everything!"

A few more dating sites were soon added to the mix, and swiping left and right became my primary form of entertainment.

The digital mania of dating apps was years away when Carole and I met in 1986. Love 'em or hate 'em, they were the primary way to meet people in the twenty-first century, particularly during a pandemic. "The dance," as I called the process of swiping, connecting, and telling the same stories over and over, had its own choreography that grew tiresome quickly.

I dated a lot, and I mean *a lot*. I ate out every night and rarely dined alone, so do the math. My monthly credit card statement looked like I was taking every unattached woman in North Texas out for a nice meal.

Because I'd started dating a few months after Carole's death, lived in a cool apartment, and ate out a lot, some women called me a player, which I thought was hilarious. An overweight, middle-aged, widowed father of special needs kids did not fit my stereotype of a hound. Being a player may have been the lifestyle some guys wanted, but not me. The goal was to find a permanent, long-term companion, and the only way to do that was to meet people. It was a numbers game, and the odds improved with the more women I met.

I DATED A LOT, AND I MEAN *A LOT*. I ATE OUT
EVERY NIGHT AND RARELY DINED ALONE,
SO DO THE MATH.

Frequent dating, combined with God's sense of humor, led to some funny moments. I met a very nice flight attendant who, for our first date, came to dinner in Legacy West, a place she'd never been. After a few dates, I thought she might be someone to focus on exclusively, but at that moment, we were still meeting other people.

Late one Saturday afternoon, I met a real estate agent for a beverage at an Italian restaurant below the Corner Suite. We had a nice conversation, the beverage evolved into dinner, and a few hours later, we walked out.

The real estate agent and I weren't three steps out the door when we got run over by the flight attendant! A missile strike would not have been that precise. She'd come for a concert with friends, and their path put them on a collision course with us, thirty feet below my apartment. Not surprisingly, she sent me a text the next day and wished me well. I later wondered if God was protecting me from her or her from me!

My relationship coach was in her mid-twenties. We knew each other well, and I could pay her in mimosas. Daddy-daughter dates with Blaire lasted four hours on a weeknight, and with her mom gone, she was the only real friend I had. She was married, and I was going out with a different woman every night, so at times it was hard to tell who was the parent and who was the child. One night, my twenty-four-year-old offered this wisdom:

"Daddy, when you meet people, there are three things you need to look out for," she started. "The first is emotional availability. Are they over whatever it is they need to be over? Second is physical availability. Do they have time in their calendar to date? The last is reciprocity. Are they pouring as much into you as you are into them? If the answer is no to any of these questions, then you need to keep looking."

Blaire's insight was perfect. Many ladies were not over their past relationships and needed to deal with their pain. It often manifested by assuming that every man, including me, was as big an asshole as their last guy, and I grew to resent that. There were classless guys out there, but I refused to pay the price for another man's sins.

A lot of women on the dating circuit didn't have time to date, and I wondered why they were meeting people at all. Some had children at home, and I respected that, but my social life would not be dictated by someone else's divorce decree.

"You're selfish and unfair to the women you meet," one lady scolded me on a dating app. "You need to get over your ex-wife and wait at least a year before meeting someone else," she lectured with obnoxious conviction.

"I don't have an ex-wife; I have a late wife," was my stern reply. Carole and I worked very hard not to have or be an "ex." Advocacy taught me that everyone views life through the lens of their own experience. I had no insight into divorce, and few people understood that the death of a spouse was different for every person.

ADVOCACY TAUGHT ME THAT EVERYONE
VIEWS LIFE THROUGH THE LENS OF
THEIR OWN EXPERIENCE.

"I was reluctant to meet you," one woman shared. "I once dated a widower. Two years after his wife's death, her clothes were still in their closet, and her robe hung on the bathroom door."

"Everyone has a right to grieve however they wish," I replied, "but that seems odd. If it makes you feel any better, all of Carole's clothes were out of the house a week after she died." To move forward, I had to put some things in the past and send others to the second-hand store.

"I don't think you're over your wife," another said as we sat on her couch. "You still have the furniture you bought with her."

"I bought it because I liked it," was my reply. "Why should I give it up? Where did you get your furniture?"

"My ex-boyfriend bought it for me," she said, obviously missing the irony in that statement.

"You don't need to take them to a nice restaurant on the first date," a friend of mine advised. "Meet 'em at Starbucks to see if they're worth it." He was working on his third divorce.

"I don't like meeting at Starbucks," I explained. "It's not comfortable for long conversations, and I want to see how they handle their liquor."

"Would you like some wine?" I usually asked on the first date. Most said yes and had four glasses to my half. It was fun to watch how I became more interesting as dinner progressed.

First glass: She would loosen up and smile at my goofy observations of life.

Second glass: My surprising candor and salaciously funny innuendos made her laugh easily.

Third glass: She freely shared things she claimed to tell no one else.

Fourth glass: I was by far the nicest guy she had ever met.

Another benefit of restaurant-first dates was pressure-testing an important issue to see how she would respond. I'd said a brief blessing over every nonbusiness meal for decades, and that didn't change on date night. I would thank God for our meal and my guest, verbally appreciating the work He had done in her life. After more than a few prayers, I would open my eyes and see a small tear in the eye of my date.

"I expect a man to be consistent," a female friend told me. "If he starts out bringing me flowers on every date, I expect that to continue. If he sends me a text every morning, he better not stop. Consistency means that I'm important to him."

"That makes no sense at all!" I replied. "Courting women at the beginning of a relationship has been around since Neanderthals lived in caves. Relationships evolve. If it evolves well, the elements of courting change into things more meaningful. Also, if you want to be spoiled forever, that's fine, but what are you doing to deserve it?"

Apparently, my tact needed work because we didn't talk for a while after that.

"The Three-Date Rule," reported by many women, was the expectation some men had of seeing them naked by the third date, or there wouldn't be a fourth. Those guys must have had a sex-to-dinner ratio, a quid pro quo for a Caesar salad. I always thought dating meant going to a restaurant or movie, not messing up the sheets.

My own Three-Date Rule soon developed:

Date 1: See if we could sit at the same table and not throw up on each other.

Date 2: Always fun, as we would go to a nice restaurant or a concert and have a good time.

Date 3: "It" would come out if it had not already. Almost every woman, and possibly I as well, had an "it," a personality trait or looming previous experience that made me think, *Uh oh.*

Here are a few examples of "its" that came out within the first three dates:

- "I've been married three times. Well, there was a fourth, but it only lasted a month, so I don't count it." I guess he figured it out faster than the others.

- "After my divorce, I would go out of town every weekend. My oldest was thirteen and would watch the younger ones." She had curious decision-making skills.
- "I'm going to text you my picture." She needed the lesson I taught Blaire as a teenager; under no circumstances should a working camera and your naked body be in the same room at the same time.
- "Let's order another bottle." That was our third, and my date was the only one drinking.
- "My husband and I have been separated for two years. Hopefully the divorce will be final soon." This was much more common than I expected.
- "I fell for a guy who said he was divorced, then after five months, he told me he was still married. We dated for another month before we broke up." I felt bad for her up until the last sentence.
- "You're nice but could use some polish. You need a new wardrobe, and you don't eat well. Also, if you want to date a woman like me, maybe you should lose weight." This was on our first date.

WE GUARANTEE SIX-TO-EIGHT DATES *with high-quality women,* read the Facebook ad. I would try almost anything once, so I clicked, filled out a form, and ten minutes later got an email. After a brief exchange online, the salesperson called.

"We interview the ladies to make sure they meet our criteria," she explained quite convincingly. "These are all professional women, not gold diggers."

"There's not much gold to dig, but that will make my oldest daughter happy," I replied. "What do you charge?"

"Your time is valuable, and we make sure you're not wasting it," she answered.

"Uh-huh. How much?" I asked again.

"You need to view it as an investment in your future. After all, she may be the next Mrs. Boatright," the saleswoman deflected again.

"Lady, you are good," I laughed, "but this conversation is about to get real short. What's your darn price?"

"Dates with six-to-eight outstanding ladies is $3,500," she reluctantly replied.

"Thanks," I said, choking on my Diet Coke, "but I can find six women to reject me for a lot less than that!"

About six weeks later, I received a message on LinkedIn from a woman at the same dating service. I responded that I had spoken with her colleague and would pass. She emailed back, "No, you spoke to someone in Sales. I'm on the matching side, and there's no cost to you at all."

She saw my profile and thought I should meet her female client. The client paid the fee, so all I had to do was show up.

"In other words, you're pimping me out?" I asked with a smile.

"I wouldn't call it that," she replied.

"I'm flattered!" I told her. "Out of curiosity, who picks up the dinner tab?"

"Sometimes they split it, but most often the man picks it up."

"Of course we do. So much for the no cost part of this deal," I clarified.

The agency picked a restaurant near the Corner Suite. Soon after I arrived, a lovely woman walked in and talked nonstop for over three hours. I had never been so excited to pick up a check to make an evening end.

AFTER A FEW DATES WITH MARY, a nice woman with expensive tastes, we decided to move on but remained friends. A few months after our last night out, her best friend called.

"Hi Clay, I want to get your thoughts," she opened. "Mary's birthday is in a few weeks. You know how sweet and generous she is."

"Yes, I do," I replied.

"Our girls' group would like to throw her a fun party," the friend continued, "but we can't do it at the level she deserves. We were wondering if you would like to pay for it."

I almost dropped the phone. It was rare for me to be at a loss for words, but I was speechless.

After a moment to crystalize my thoughts, I replied, "Let me make sure I have this straight. You want me to pay for a birthday party I can't attend for someone I saw three times and am no longer dating. Is that right?" The perplexity in my voice was obvious.

A few seconds later, she responded, "Well, it doesn't sound very nice when you put it that way. Let me know what you want to do. Bye!" I didn't call her back.

"QUIT TAKING WOMEN TO THE COWBOYS CLUB," a friend advised.

"Why? I'm there all the time, and it's a nice place to talk," I replied.

"Clay, you're flexing too soon," he said. I had no idea what he meant.

The club staff offered to screen my victims, so it became a first or second-date event. Sometimes conversations would go long, and we'd be the last ones there when the vacuum cleaners fired up. One evening after servers Steve and Kassie stayed late because of me, I sent Steve an apology and thanked them for their graciousness.

He replied, "It was our pleasure, Clay. We're all your wingmen."

Whether by design or coincidence, Steve was our server for at least 70 percent of my dates at the club. He had an unobstructed line of sight into my private life better than I did.

"Yeah, she wasn't your type. No need to repeat," Steve mentioned one afternoon, referring to a woman I'd brought in a few nights earlier. Folks in the hospitality industry learned to read people quickly, and I appreciated him catching things I didn't.

EVERY ADULT HAS STUFF, the difficulties that make our lives unique. Heck, you're reading a book about mine! My goal was not to find a woman who had no challenges but someone who could manage them.

"Everyone has experiences and challenges, baggage, and drama," one woman told me.

"Yes and no," I replied. "We all have experiences and challenges, but baggage and drama are optional. Those come from our attitudes and how we choose to look at our lives. Happiness is a choice."

Advocacy with special needs parents prepared me for dating in several ways. Every story was unique, including some that made my world look normal. Pain and disappointment were the focus for many, and they wanted everyone to know that their lives sucked. Soon I was telling my dates the same thing I'd tell the parents. They'd been through fire and survived thus far. God had a plan, and their attitude would determine success and happiness.

"WE ALL HAVE EXPERIENCES AND CHALLENGES, BUT BAGGAGE AND DRAMA ARE OPTIONAL."

"It's taken over six months, but I've finally figured out women," I told Blaire one night on a daddy-daughter date at the club.

"Oh, here we go," she replied as she braced herself.

"First, you're all crazy," I stated matter-of-factly.

"This is true," she agreed. Some facts could not be denied.

"Second, do you know what women really want?"

"What?" she asked.

"They want someone to care," I said slowly.

"Far and away, the most common statement women say to me is, and I'm quoting, 'I can't believe I'm telling you this.' It usually occurs between forty-five and sixty minutes into our first meeting and leads to an in-depth conversation on a sensitive topic. That's why most of my dates last until after midnight."

"So, what does that tell you?" Blaire asked.

"I'm easy to talk to, they feel respected, their opinions matter, and they're being heard. Quite simply, they want to be appreciated."

That's when it hit me. Our lives are made up of relationships. Whether it be husband-wife, parent-child, boss-employee, or bartender-customer, there's one thing all of us want from all our relationships—to be appreciated.

But maybe appreciation is more than the key to relationships, with an even larger role in our lives. During the chaos of raising our children, I appreciated that I had a family to love and support—a wife and daughters who loved and depended on me. After Carole died, I appreciated the years we'd had together and that she was now in the arms of God. In the craziness of dating, I appreciated that people wanted to get to know me and that I could navigate that very different and sometimes awkward world.

Every day, I find something to appreciate, and I let people know how important they are. It's made all the difference.

APPENDIX

BOOK CLUB STUDY QUESTIONS

1. Carole and Clay left their hometown, family, and friends early in their marriage. As a result, they had no support network or help when the challenges hit. What are your thoughts about starting a new life from scratch in a new place? Describe your support network and who you turn to for help.

2. Clay's father taught him that second-guessing and asking *"What if?"* was a waste of time. Think about times you've second-guessed a decision. Why did you do that? What was the result of those thoughts?

3. Several times, Clay and Carole battled medical and educational authorities. What do you expect from experts on topics you know little about? Describe a time you disagreed with an expert and how you handled it.

4. Receiving Paige and Mia's disability diagnosis was a pivotal moment for the Boatrights. Think about a time you and your partner were faced with an unexpected problem. How did you respond?

5. Clay believed his twins' disabilities were part of God's plan. Do you believe God creates or allows challenges for

a specific purpose? Describe a challenge you believe God meant for you to endure and why.

6. God gave Clay insight into the twins during his Friday Night Revelation and again about his future in the Tom Thumb grocery store after Carole's death. Has God provided you with clarity on a tough situation? How did you respond?

7. Clay and Carole watched Paige wither away, almost to the point of death, with significant behavior and personality changes. Think about a time you felt hopeless. How did you get through it?

8. People react to tragedies differently. One husband kept his late wife's bathrobe hanging on their door for years after she died, while Clay donated Carole's clothes and sold their house as soon as he could. How do you think you would respond to a significant loss, like that of a spouse or child?

9. Everyone has an identity, how others know them. Clay's identity came from his family and disability advocacy, not his employer. Where does your identity come from? How do your identity and priorities line up with where you spend your time?

10. Do you believe happiness is the result of specific circumstances or a choice in how we respond? What is the source of your happiness, and how often is it achieved?

11. The end of the book talks about the importance of feeling appreciated. Do you feel appreciated by the people in your life? How do you show your appreciation for others?

ABOUT THE AUTHOR

A native of Memphis, Tennessee, Clay Boatright has lived in Texas since 1994, where he and his wife Carole raised three daughters, including identical twins with severe intellectual disabilities and autism. With undergrad and graduate degrees from the University of Memphis, Clay managed two full-time careers for almost twenty years, one in the consumer-packaged goods industry to pay the bills and another as a volunteer advocate for people with disabilities.

Over the years, Clay developed a deep understanding of the disability industrial complex and served on a host of health and education advisory committees, including Board President for both The Arc of Dallas and The Arc of Texas. In 2011, President Barack Obama appointed Clay to the President's Committee for People with Intellectual Disabilities in Washington, DC, and in 2013, he was appointed Founding Chairman for Texas Health & Human Services' IDD System Redesign Advisory Committee, which he held for six years. Published multiple times in various media, Clay is often contacted by legislators, the media, nonprofit organizations, and parents of children with disabilities to help understand the challenges that families like his live every day.

Following Carole's death in 2020 from ovarian cancer, Clay maintains a close relationship with his daughters and embraces the future with enthusiasm and a desire to help everyone know that God has a plan for their lives. His personal motto is "Life is too important to be taken seriously!"

To learn more, check out www.clayboatright.com
or www.GodsPlanOurCircus.com.

CPSIA information can be obtained
at www.ICGtesting.com
Printed in the USA
LVHW102032210123
737679LV00003B/19

9 781955 711227